The Forgiveness Factor

Living Beyond the Pain of Your Past

A True Story of Hope and Perseverance

Scott Bradley

The Forgiveness Factor
Living Beyond the Pain of Your Past

Copyright 2012 by Scott Bradley

ISBN 978-0-9839993-4-8

Printed in the United States of America

ALL RIGHTS RESERVED

Editor: Linda Dodge

www.theforgivenessfactor.com

Published by
Pure Desire Ministries International
Gresham, Oregon
www.puredesire.org

July 2012

Dedicated to Gwenna,
my wife, best friend, and soul mate:
Without you, this book isn't possible.

CONTENTS

INTRODUCTION

"Forgiveness is the answer to the child's dream of a miracle by which what is broken is made whole again, what is soiled is made clean again."
Dag Hammarskjold

On the morning I began writing this book our family was making plans to visit Disneyland. We had reserved our tickets and mapped out our trip. We were going to stop along the way to see my dad, sisters, and extended family. We made all the preparations to make it a wonderful trip to the happiest place on earth. The family accompanying me included my wife of eleven years, Gwenna, our two beautiful daughters, eight-year-old Maicee, five-year-old Sophie, and our niece, Mariah. At this writing, my girls are still at the age where they believe they are princesses. I feel extremely blessed to have them in my life.

As I began writing, I realized that exactly twenty years ago, I was sitting in the Klamath County Jail, convicted of felony assault. I was responsible for almost beating a young man to death. At 17 years of age, I was facing a long prison term, and scared to death. I was in serious trouble and spent my 18th birthday alone in a jail cell feeling hopeless, worthless, and alone.

How did my life go so terribly wrong? What happened to the little boy who dreamt of being a pastor? What happened to the young man that was good at sports and excelled in mathematics? What happened to my innocence? Why was I filled with rage and anger? To where did my gentle and soft spirit flee?

Furthermore, how could this young man ever forgive me? What would his family believe about the "reckless thug" that did such a horrible thing to their beloved? How could I look in the mirror and not see a beast? How could I ever get past my past? I believed I was destined to a life of imprisonment, institutions, and regret. What could possibly change in my heart to help me see the "real me"? Most people had already written me off, while others approved of my incarceration. Other people's judgments reinforced the negative self-image I carried inside. I believed I had no value, and nothing to offer this world.

I've always had the willingness, but often doubted my ability to change. Permanent change takes time and perseverance. Each of us has a choice. We can be enslaved to our past, or live in freedom as a people liberated. We do not have to live as victims or survivors of the past; we are more than conquerors in Jesus Christ. We can move beyond betrayal, disappointment, abandonment, abuse, and loss. It begins with addressing and owning the trauma we carry in our souls.

Everyone has wounds that keep them from experiencing healthy relationships. The wounds are like an anchor keeping a vessel attached within a harbor of pain. The vessel is designed to sail the high seas, moving on the waves of love and liberty. The forgiveness factor enables us to remove our unhealthy attachments and receive the blessing of renewed relationships. The primary goal of this book is to initiate the healing of those heart wounds.

This is a raw and authentic reflection of my life. I don't write as a man who has "arrived," nor have I perfected every healing principle. I openly admit that I am challenged with feeling comfortable in my own skin. Feeling inferior has always haunted me. I often feel like I do not measure up to those around me. I am not sure how to explain it. Maybe those who have felt alone in a crowd, experienced isolation in churches full of people, or spent endless days internalizing their pain will understand. Is that you?

If you have felt this way, then maybe you know what I am talking about. In response to this pain and loneliness, I tend to self-medicate. This self-medication has revealed itself in people pleasing, unhealthy relationships, sexual escapades, overworking, substance abuse, overeating, codependency, gambling, and religiosity. I have spent the past year processing an extreme amount of pain, grief, and loss. I thought I lost my dreams and blamed everyone else for my poor choices. I need to forgive. I need to be forgiven. I want to live with passion and purpose again.

I must admit, I've felt extremely vulnerable while writing this book. I am afraid of being viewed as a fraud or hypocrite. My anxiety and fear is rooted in the way I've dealt with life. I still struggle with trusting God, others, and myself. I still wrestle with unforgiveness, resentment, and anger. I believe I have grown in many ways, but in others, still act like a child. The Apostle Paul encourages us to put our childish ways behind us as we become adults (1 Corinthians 13:11).

The truth is that we are all created in God's image (Genesis 3), and God's heart is one of restoration. He longs for us to be restored into the image of His son, Jesus Christ. My experience in life, relationships, marriage, family, ministry, and counseling hurting people has shown me that forgiveness is misunderstood. The basics of forgiveness and reconciliation seem to be marred by cynicism and doubt. Personally, I've said I have forgiven people and then let resentment and contempt towards them control my life. I have heard countless people react in anger and hatred against the very people they say they have forgiven. Is that forgiveness? How can a person "let go" of the hurtful things said, done, and experienced? How do we become "empowered" to set others and ourselves free?

I have lived most of my life holding onto the past, being angry with others, and questioning God's divine authority. I also spent a great deal of energy and emotion filled with shame from the pain and hurt I have caused others. How can I move on from abuse, abandonment, neglect, and pain? How do I make amends to those I have damaged? How can I be forgiven?

Where does forgiveness fit into my life? Who could possibly give me hope and a future? What would eventually become of my life?

The book you are about to read is a dangerous book. I say that because faith involves fear. We must step out in faith to trust others. We must step out in faith to forgive our trespassers. I've been challenged to dig deep in seeing the truth about my experiences. This included spending time with my parents and re-visiting the painful memories of our family's past, while sharing emotional conversations with friends and family. I am convinced that God has a greater plan in mind for us. It goes beyond becoming the "Bradley Bunch." It is a call to help hurting individuals and families find healing.

This book will challenge you to re-think your ability to forgive. It will point you to Jesus Christ, the Forgiveness Factor. He is the one who can empower you to go beyond your own abilities and strength. Jesus is not a joint smoking, feather-haired, free spirit wandering through a pasture cuddling a lamb. He is God's only Son and on a mission to free humankind. He came offering forgiveness by giving His life in our place. He is the Forgiveness Factor.

Through writing this book, my hope is to find a deeper maturity in walking with God and others. Will you join me in this journey to understanding forgiveness?

one

IN THE BEGINNING

"Honor your father and mother
Which is the first commandment with a promise
so that it may go well with you..
that you may enjoy long life on the earth."
Ephesians 6:2-3

Parents play a major role influencing the lives of their children and impact their kids in every possible aspect. Children learn if the world is safe or dangerous, how to relate to others, and develop personality traits under their parents' care. Kids learn discipline and structure. They learn how to live life and become adults.

Lack of healthy parents can deeply confuse and wound a child. Some symptoms or behaviors of wounded children might be: escalated rebellion, nightmares, inattentiveness (ADD/ADHD), and preoccupation with daydreaming, hostility, and aggression. These kids learn early on to blame, minimize, deny, and manipulate. They also develop trust and intimacy issues. If not addressed, these internal issues can grow into full-blown emotional/mental disorders.

I am writing this book with my parents. They have shared their stories with me, and I would like to share them with you. It will help you get the "big picture" and see how transformation is possible. Hopefully, our story will give you a chance to reflect on your journey and how your life was shaped through the generations before you.

My dad has always been a hero to me. His life today represents the power of forgiveness and the offer of real life through faith in Jesus Christ. God's love was perfect in giving me this man as a father and brother in Christ. My mom is an amazing woman. She is the embodiment of love. I have experienced the love of God through her since the day of my birth. She has given sacrificially, loved endlessly, and served tirelessly. She is a courageous woman representing the love of Jesus Christ. When God placed me in her hands, He knew I would be blessed for eternity!

Our family, like most families, struggled through disappointment, mistakes, and dysfunction. We had plenty of challenges and not much support. Most kids expect perfection and idealize their parents. I was no different. Although I did not understand all of the obstacles facing my parents, I never stopped loving them. However, I would spend a good part of my life full of anger, rage, and carrying resentment towards God, my parents, and anyone who had harmed me.

I did not understand why my parents divorced or why I was subjected to abuse. I did not understand why people would abandon those they loved. I did not understand why people would say one thing, yet do another. From an early age, I lost all respect for authority and learned to protect myself at all costs. I internalized most of my feelings and felt entitled to live as I pleased. In my world, it was an eye for an eye and tooth for a tooth.

It was not long before I became what I had resented: a destructive, drug addicted, rage-aholic. I did not see value in others or myself. These feelings only escalated as time went on. There was an enormous wake of hostility and devastation flowing straight from the propeller of my destructive lifestyle. It was not until I embraced the forgiveness factor that my life began to change.

Dad's family of origin

"He will restore the hearts of the fathers to their children and the hearts of the children to their fathers..."
Malachi 4:6

My dad was born in Oklahoma to my grandfather and his first wife, a full-blooded Cherokee Indian. Within a couple months of his birth, his mother died of pancreatic cancer. This was a difficult transition for my grandfather. He was responsible for raising my dad and his older sister without a mother. That's when he decided to move his family to California to live with his mother. He thought she could help take care of the kids while he tried to figure out what to do with his life. While living there my grandfather met his second wife. She would become my dad's "mommy" and give birth to three more children. They remained married until my grandfather's death.

My grandfather was a self-employed World War II veteran who struggled with alcoholism. Work was hard to find and the family lived in poverty. Many evenings my Dad and his siblings would pick up cans along the highway to help put food on the table. At one point, they were staying in a house with dirt floors, no electricity, and no running water.

As a boy, Dad learned the value of hard work. When he wanted to buy something, he had to earn it. He bucked hay and worked at a dairy to buy his first bicycle. When he was in his early teens, they moved to Klamath Falls, Oregon.

Upon entering high school, he started thinking about his future. He was not satisfied with the life his family lived: broke, dysfunctional, and impoverished. He was at the age when young men begin searching for their identity and seeking independence. This search led him to develop a pattern of drinking and fighting with his buddies. My dad longed to settle down and raise a family, while working hard towards building a different life, full of promise. Life presented many options, but his call to serve was evident.

After several of his friends joined the Marines, Dad enlisted in 1968. The Vietnam War was in full swing and serving his country presented an opportunity to prove his manhood and challenge his fears. He felt proud to personally join and not be drafted by one of the other armed services. In his mind, he knew what it meant to be a Marine. They were the "real men" who stood on the front lines without fear, and fought to the death. He knew in his heart that the Marines did the "real fighting."

Madly in love, he promised his girlfriend they would marry when he returned from Vietnam. They planned to meet in Hawaii to share their vows of marriage. At this point in life, things had meaning and purpose. It appeared his dreams had come true and he would fulfill his plans for a family.

Mom's family of origin

"I am reminded of your sincere faith, which first lived in your grandmother.... and in your mother... and, I am persuaded, now lives in you also."

2 Timothy 1:5-6

Mom and three siblings were raised in Klamath Falls by my grandmother and her stepdad (my grandpa John). Grandpa adopted her at an early age and he was her "daddy." He was a godly man who worked hard at the local lumber mill. He was a recovering alcoholic, and prayed for his family every day. My grandmother was a beautiful woman who loved her family.

My grandmother had previously been abandoned by a couple of men. This led to divorce and pain for her. One of them was Mom's biological father. He left my grandma for another woman shortly after my mom's birth.

Since my grandmother's family condemned divorce, she struggled to find acceptance and love from her own family. In addition, it was not culturally acceptable to be divorced in her generation. She carried deep pain and shame from her life experiences. Her simple goal in life was to be a good mother and be loved by a caring man. Then God strategically placed John in her life. They went to church every Sunday and were encouraged to live a godly life. The kids all attended public schools and were a positive influence in the community.

Mom, an especially sensitive and shy person, was attractive both inside and out. She learned to love Jesus at a young age and accepted Him as Lord and Savior. She had many wonderful experiences growing up with her siblings. However, one of the dark times was a visit to her grandparent's house. It was on this occasion that her grandfather sexually abused her. This was very traumatic and left her questioning herself. Like her mother, she began carrying a heavy load of shame and insecurity. Her self-image was negatively shaped by the abuse. With her innocence betrayed, she now lived with self-rejection and pain, and her self worth plummeted. She felt an unhealthy vulnerability with authority figures and men.

Mom carried these feelings through school and into young adulthood. Despite being insecure, she was outgoing and found temporary relief in partying with friends. It was at a party that she first met my Dad, who was one of her brother's friends.

From then on, Mom and Dad occasionally saw each other at parties and social gatherings. They never dated in high school, but she knew he was one of the town's eligible bachelors. She learned he was deployed to Vietnam and did not see him until he returned. He came home a different man.

Personal reflection on the childhood experiences of my parents

Before writing this book, I rarely took time trying to understand the difficulties that my parents faced as they grew up. I never took into consideration that their families and experiences helped shape their lives. I have also had time to reflect on the role of my grandparents who also faced many challenges and painful choices in trying to raise families. Despite having dreams and aspirations to make a positive difference for the next generation, they had their own troubles and emotional wounds.

My Dad

My Mom

two

WOUNDS OF WAR

"You see, at just the right time, when we were still powerless, Christ died for the ungodly... But God demonstrates his own love for us in this: While we were still sinners, Christ died for us."
Romans 5:6-8

My dad was proud and excited to join the Marines. He left for boot camp with big dreams and a heart to serve his country. During boot camp he realized he was not as tough as he thought he was. The path set before him was one that would take courage, strength, and honor. He was ready to put his life on the line, fighting for freedom. Even though he enjoyed hard work, he was about to be changed. He was a small town boy venturing into a living hell. After completing boot camp, he was trained as a radioman.

While preparing for war, he began drinking and partying heavily. On one occasion, he went to the beach with his fellow servicemen. They partied hard and most of them passed out drunk on the beach. There he met a hippie girl. She invited him to hang out with her group of friends. Since he was more of a redneck, things did not go so well. They ended up in a huge brawl, which left my dad hospitalized. The next day his fellow Marines heard what

Dad in his Dress Blues

happened and went back to settle the score. This was the first of many such events for my dad.

Shortly after radio school, he proudly wore his uniform home on leave to Klamath Falls. It was an honor to be a Marine and he carried the responsibility proudly. After his home visit, he went to Okinawa for a few weeks, where he first tried smoking pot.

His next assignment was in South Vietnam. This operation involved joining a nighttime patrol unit. His assignments were extremely frightening, as men were dying in the dark of night. The jungle was eerily quiet, except for the sound of firearms, bombs, and the screams of wounded men. He knew that each step could be his last since there were booby traps everywhere.

During one of his expeditions, he experienced bombs exploding all around him. His group of soldiers had traveled down a dark trail and he ended up standing on top of a 250-pound bomb. The bomb never detonated, but eighteen of his fellow marines were wounded or lost their lives.

Some of these men were his close friends, like brothers. It was a massacre. He was one of the few young men that made it out alive. It is extremely traumatic to lose your close friends, let alone, in this manner. He believes that God was protecting him. For his courageous and valiant effort, he received the Vietnam Cross of Gallantry, Purple Heart, and Bronze Star V. The Bronze Star with combat V is for heroism. It was an honor to receive those medals, but he would have given anything to have his brothers back.

An even deeper wound broke his heart. While he was recovering, he received a "Dear John" letter from his sweetheart. She informed him that she found another man. She would not be waiting for his return. That letter was the atomic bomb that shredded his soul. He could take the casualties of war, but to lose the love of his life killed him. It destroyed his dream of settling down and raising a family. Many of his friends came home in boxes; he came home a different man.

Upon returning to the United States, he longed to taste the sweet freedom it had to offer. He says if you have ever tasted freedom and been in places where it is not present, you will fight for it. He joined the Marines, fought for freedom, and returned home anticipating a warm welcome, full of honor and appreciation. He served his country and fought for the freedom of many people. He was filled with excitement as the plane touched down back in the states. He couldn't wait to step foot on American soil. The Marines identified him as a hero and treated him with honor. When he exited the plane he wasn't met with honor and respect, only hostile protestors. They spit on him, hurled slanderous accusations at him, and called him "Baby Killer." It seemed he was a hated man, and that added insult to injury. He also found it extremely difficult to receive the benefits the government had promised veterans. It did not make sense that he would literally lay down his life, and then his country would not follow through on their commitments. He grew to hate the government for this.

When Dad arrived home, he was not the simple, innocent young man who left for war. He had experienced deep pain and emotional wounds. The depth of his trauma would soon surface in all of his relationships. He became engulfed in using alcohol, drugs, and sex to mask his pain. He did not realize these choices were anesthetics for the pain in his heart. It was the beginning of a long and destructive season in his life.

At that time, my mom had just returned to Klamath Falls after living in Phoenix, Arizona. She witnessed several of her friends come home from the war; some of them were alive and others arrived in caskets. She remembers attending the funeral for one of the young men. This was a confusing time for her. She was a young girl, barely out of high school, looking for a man she could believe in.

She re-connected with my Dad and fell in love with him. She thought he was handsome and strong. He bought a maroon 1967 Camaro and lived as he pleased. He was twenty years old. She was eighteen. My mom was attracted to everything about him. He worked hard and carried an attitude. She noticed he drank a lot since returning home, but that would change if married, so she thought. They started hanging out and he asked for her hand in marriage. It seemed like the perfect situation. They both had dreams and aspirations to settle down and start a family.

In 1970, they married in Reno, Nevada. The trip was a drunken blur and my Dad was caught stealing whiskey on their wedding night. To complicate things further, they took Mom's best friend with them. She was a young woman that my dad had also slept with. Their marriage was instant chaos.

My dad was thankful he had a wife and was still alive, but he had no idea how his past was still affecting him. He continued drinking and abusing everything in his life. His motto was drugs, women, and rock n' roll. He was on a serious path of destruction, and now my Mom was along for the ride. He was young and wanted to change, but the memories of death and destruction continued to haunt him. He would have done anything to erase the thoughts, pictures, voices, and agony that consumed him.

He turned into a very dark person, but Mom still loved him. She became pregnant and lost their first child through a miscarriage. Even though he repeatedly hurt her, she believed he was a good person. There were many times he beat her, abused her, and treated her the way he viewed himself. In response to his sin and shame, he partied harder, trying to outrun the past. She felt extremely alone and afraid as his destructive behavior escalated. Eventually Mom became pregnant again, excited to be a mother. She hoped this would help my dad "settle down." Her childhood dream soon turned into a nightmare.

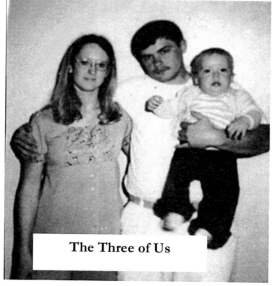

The Three of Us

She went into labor in May of 1973. My grandmother was there to support my Mom during my birth. But Dad was not around; he was out partying. Mom didn't understand why he wouldn't want to be present at his first son's birth. His choices didn't make any sense. Dad was proud to be a father. However, that did not change his reckless lifestyle or addictive behavior. His seemingly uncontrollable behavior led to him raping my Mom's sister while she babysat me.

My grandparents grew to hate him. At first they encouraged Mom to try to make things work, but his erratic behavior strained their support. Mom left him and returned to their home. When he found out she left, he went to their house, with gun in hand, and threatened to kill all of them. His violent behavior increased along with his use of drugs, alcohol, and pills.

His destructive behavior came to a head one Sunday afternoon. After spending the day drinking, he was involved in a barroom brawl in which another man lost his life. Dad left the scene, and went back to my parents' trailer covered in blood. My mom was completely terrified. He took off his clothes and demanded that she wash off the blood. She argued with him, and his friends eventually threw the clothes on the roof of the trailer next door. At midnight, police cars surrounded their trailer park and demanded his surrender. They had the entire community blocked off. During the arrest, one of the officers snatched me from my mom's arms and demanded he confess to the murder or they would never see me again. After a brief argument, they took him to jail. My Mom was traumatized and left wondering what to do with her life. She was scared, lonely, and confused.

He was charged with murder. My mom was heartbroken and did not know if she would see him again. Alone, she walked through the agonizing experience of supporting him during the proceedings of the trial. She sat with the victim's family and listened to their pain of losing a loved one. She had to view all of the bloody pictures and see the family's tears. Her heart broke for everyone involved. After going through the grueling trial, Dad was convicted of manslaughter and sentenced to 10 years in the Oregon State Penitentiary. The judge, stated, "Your sentence is 10 years, but I wish I could give you life." At that point Dad was led out of the courtroom and taken to the Oregon State Penitentiary. The judge's words cut deep. When Dad returned from Vietnam, he experienced angry faces and the disgust of war protesters; this felt like a similar experience. This, obviously, put a strain on their marriage. It made a difficult situation almost unbearable. He tried sharing his story with government officials, even writing the President, but no one would respond. My Mom took me to see him in prison and also fought for his release. She truly believed he could be a responsible man and a loving father. She saw the good in a wounded and confused young man. She practically begged the parole board for his release.

Finally, a state legislator took up his cause and Dad was released from prison six months later. Upon release, he quickly returned to his old behaviors. The pain of the past never left him, it only led to further pain for those around him. His trauma was deep and no one could take away the memories.

Man Dead In Fight At Tavern

James Edwin Carland, 30, 1008 Owens St., was killed in a fight at the Midway Tavern, eight miles south of Klamath Falls on Highway 39, Sunday night when it is believed by police he was beaten and hit on the head with a bar stool.

Later Sunday night, Anthony James Bardley, 23, 5001 Miller Ave., was arrested and lodged at the Klamath County Jail on a

Newspaper Article 1974

My mom finally had the courage to leave him; they were divorced in 1974. She realized you can't love an addict out of their addiction. She believes our entire family was a casualty of the Vietnam War. She was now traumatized and wounded in ways she would not understand until later in life.

> *"They are darkened in their understanding and separated from the life of God because of the ignorance that is in them due to the hardening of their hearts. Having lost all sensitivity, they have given themselves over to sensuality so as to indulge in every kind of impurity, with a continual lust for more."*
>
> Ephesians 4:18-19

I cannot begin to understand or feel the misery my parents must have been living in. How do people return from a war where death and destruction are a daily experience and not be traumatized? How does a person process those experiences? PTSD (post traumatic stress disorder) is a real condition affecting countless numbers of veterans. I am not letting my dad off the hook for his destructive choices, but he does carry many traumatic experiences within him.

I do not know why good things happen to bad people, or why bad things happen to good people. It does not make sense that they both had good intentions, yet they wound up being enslaved to their pasts. I will never fully understand the trauma Dad experienced in Vietnam. I cannot comprehend the pain and agony Mom faced in trying to love him in his destructive state. How was transformation or healing a possibility for my parents? It causes many questions to arise in my mind.

- Where was God in all of this?
- How can someone be healed from such tragedy?
- Where do people turn when wounded so deeply?
- What about the children?
- Could my Dad ever be forgiven for all the pain and anguish he caused others?

If you're interested in discovering how your family history is affecting you, I would recommend starting with a genogram. A genogram is a way to examine your family tree by looking at your family members and their relationships over two to three generations. Take time to write out different characteristics like:

- How did they handle conflict?
- How did they parent their children?
- Did they experience trauma?
- What kinds of addictions run in your family?
- How well did your family talk about feelings?

This will help you address some of the possible "sticking points" in your life. Sticking points are old memories or behaviors that you can't move beyond.

If these exercises bring a lot of pain to the surface, please find a qualified counselor or pastor to help process your feelings.

"It is freeing to become aware that we don't have to be victims of our past and can learn new ways of responding. But there is a step beyond this recognition... It is the step of forgiveness. Forgiveness is love practiced among people who love poorly. It sets us free without wanting anything in return."

Henri Nouwen

Pete Bradley joined the Marines and was deployed to Vietnam in July 1969.

1969-70: HIS YEAR IN VIETNAM

Pete Bradley spent a year — from July 1969 to July 1970 — on the front lines in Vietnam.

His duties involved medevac and radio support, so he called in airstrikes that likely killed many.

He only remembers one time in which he stared down the end of his .45 pistol at a enemy soldier coming at him with a fixed bayonet.

He fired on the assailant, dropping him instantly. Bradley strained to catch his breath.

Bradley lost friends and fellow Marines during his 365 days in Southeast Asia.

He was wounded when his troop found themselves in a heavily booby-trapped area, bombs exploded, taking out 18 of his comrades.

He knew he was lucky that he returned home alive, not in a wooden box.

When he arrived in the U.S., protesters spat on him and called him a "baby killer," invalidating his efforts to protect his country's freedom, he said.

He brought back with him a Purple Heart, a Vietnamese Cross of Gallantry and a bronze star for valor. He also brought back PTSD, post-traumatic stress disorder.

three

SOMEBODY TO LOVE

"People ask me what advice I have for a married couple struggling in their relationship. I always answer: pray and forgive. And to young people from violent homes, I say: pray and forgive. And again, even to the single mother with no family support: pray and forgive."
Mother Teresa

In the wake of pain and trauma, Mom began a survival lifestyle. People struggling to survive are driven by fear and will self-protect at all costs. They are embedded with stress and anxiety, trusting no one. Our culture is full of people surviving, despite the abundance of resources and counseling availability. Our society is driven to medicate fear with addictions, relationships, and image-management. Living in survival and being addicted is now the "norm." This was not true for my parents' generation. My mom didn't have these resources, so she turned to another man.

Shortly after Mom divorced Dad, she met her second husband. He was not a loud, cocky, over-the-top personality like my dad. He seemed consistent, settled down, and able to give her the life she desired. They married and she became pregnant with my twin sisters, Lisa and Lori. They were born premature and barely survived. Mom loved taking care of us and wanted an intimate relationship with her husband. However, she did not understand the negative impact of her previous traumatic experiences. She struggled to love her husband, but because of her past traumas, she was not emotionally available to him. They divorced four years later.

After my parents' divorce, my dad continued his destructive behavior. He had a new girlfriend and was dealing drugs. Within a few months, he was sent back to prison on a parole violation—he punched a guy during a drug deal. This led to another three-and-a-half-year sentence.

In prison, his out-of-control behavior continued. He "snuck out" of prison, drank, had sex, and did drugs on several occasions. He would've been prosecuted for escape if caught, but it never happened. While incarcerated he married his second wife. They exchanged their wedding vows inside the prison. Upon release, my dad and his wife bought a house in Keno, a small town outside of Klamath Falls, Oregon. They continued using drugs and drinking. His wife became pregnant with my sister, Star.

I have vague memories of visiting them when my mom was married to her second husband. I recall one occasion when I placed a phone call to my Mom and her husband answered. As we spoke I called him Dad, and my dad ripped the phone out of my hand yelling, "You're my son, not anyone else's!"

That was the first time I saw him lose it. The intense anger in his face was frightening. Despite that incident, I really enjoyed visiting him. I could tell his wife really loved me as her own son, but it did not last long. When his wife left for a short trip to California, Dad found another girlfriend. He kicked his wife and my sister out, and moved the girlfriend into the house. Of course, that relationship didn't last long before he found another woman to marry.

My dad and his third wife lived together for a while before moving to Chiloquin, Oregon. They soon had a child, my sister Sada. That marriage would also end. Star, Sada, and I were growing up without our father. My Dad did not realize he had a problem; he thought everyone partied, drank, did drugs, and slept around. I believe he went from denial to delusional. Instead of denying his past and his problems, he believed he was the problem. My dad did not have a clue about how to have a healthy

My sister, Sada Bradley

relationship. He eventually married for a fourth time. That marriage ended in divorce.

more of the same for mom

After my mom divorced her second husband, she moved into her own place, taking my twin sisters and me with her. Mom worked hard as a waitress and always kept a roof over our heads. She did her best to keep the house clean, cook meals, and provided for all our needs.

After dating a few people, mom fell in love with Randy, a hard working, friendly person. They were together for three years, and he eventually told her that he did not want to marry. I will explain this further in a later chapter. Since her relationship with Randy was over, she ran into the arms of Hal, who became her third husband. He was quite a bit older and established in the community. He had a band that played in local bars, and he had been a Baptist minister earlier in his life. He was a nursing home administrator and brought stability into our lives.

One afternoon while my Mom was cleaning our house she found a box full of cassette tape recordings of Hal preaching sermons. He shared a message on the grace of God that touched her heart. He spoke about God finding value in lepers and using them for His eternal purposes. Mom wept because she felt like an outcast, and turned her life over to Jesus. She rejoiced, knowing that God could love and accept her.

It was a day that would change her life forever. She went to the church she grew up in and spoke with the pastor. He prayed over her, and she felt a renewed sense of peace in her heart. Then she drove to Hal's office and told him everything that had happened. He knew it was God moving and also gave his life back to Christ.

Mom and Hal started taking our family to church. My Mom loved Jesus and started to see hope for her family. My sisters and I were baptized. We became involved in many church activities. We moved several times--from Klamath Falls, Oregon, to Selah, Washington, to Florence, Oregon, to Mapleton, Oregon, and eventually to Lebanon, Oregon. In each of those towns, we attended a local church and served in ministry.

While we lived in Lebanon, Mom and Hal started a church. The services were fantastic with Hal preaching and leading worship. Things were going great—until Mom's best friend notified her of Hal's infidelity. There was a horrible resignation from the church. My sisters and my mom were deeply wounded—again.

Hal, my mom, and twin sisters eventually moved to Gresham, Oregon, to get help for his sexual addiction. He seemed to be getting better and was back leading worship at the church, until he became involved with another woman. Mom tried to get him to seek help, but he refused. He left with his new mistress, and Mom divorced him. Here she was again, left alone in an extreme amount of pain and wondering what to do with her life. I did not live with them at this time but it was very traumatic for my mother and sisters, who were now in high school. How could they not be deeply wounded from these experiences?

darker days ahead for dad

After my dad divorced his fourth wife, he took a turn for the worse, if that was possible. He was deeply enmeshed in doing meth and dealing drugs. He partied hard and continued acting irresponsible. Nothing could stop the pain of Vietnam, failed marriages, time spent in prison, or poor choices he had made. By 1996, he had been arrested four to five times for possession of meth. He continued to break his parole and was a wanted man.

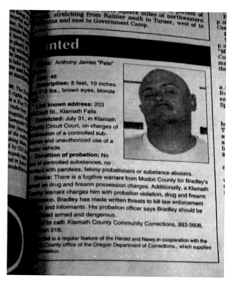

He did not want to get caught and go back to prison, so one of his African-American friends convinced him to shave his head and paint himself black. He shaved his head, bought wigs, and changed his name. This kept Dad out of jail for a while, but it just added to his deceptive lifestyle. On top of that, the woman with whom he did drugs became pregnant. During the pregnancy, Dad was arrested and put back in jail.

During this incarceration, he had an experience with God. He remembers sitting in his cell, throwing his hands in the air, and crying out to God, "Lord if you are real, I need you in my life!" As he was lying in the dark, a bright light appeared and said, "I want you to go to Texas, and build me a temple." He laid there shaking on his bed, not understanding what this meant. He had many questions and wondered what would he use for money, or what type of temple, or how could he pull together the resources to build something that big. All he heard was, "I will provide," and the light disappeared. A few weeks later, he was released and forgot all about the experience with God.

Upon release, Dad moved to Washington. He got into serious trouble selling meth, drugs, and firearms. He was working as a bodyguard for a wealthy gangster. Their business was stealing cars, motorcycles, and other valuables. It was pure greed. His boss was arrested and put in jail. Dad had a long list of warrants for his arrest. These included charges in Idaho, Oregon, Washington, and a 25-year sentence for firearms and other drug charges in California. That's when he decided to join his girlfriend in Texas. She had given birth to their son and named him Chance. He was named Chance because my Dad believed that this would be his last chance to be a father.

Dad & Chance in May 2005

While in Texas, Dad remembered the vision God had given him. He tried making positive changes, but his erratic behaviors only increased. His flashbacks grew in severity to the point of him grabbing his girlfriend by the throat, thinking she was Vietnamese.

He knew he would eventually kill her too, so he decided to get help. He went to the local VA medical center and asked for psychiatric help. He asked them for a brain transplant and they just chuckled, "We don't do those here." He said, "Listen, you don't understand, I need to get Vietnam out of my head!" They put him on some psychotropic medication, and things seemed to stabilize. Finally he had some relief from his pain. The VA helped him file for full disability and benefits. Each time he went to the Veteran's Hospital, God kept reminding him to build the temple. In response to this reminder, he would go kneel and pray at the chapel. He prayed that God would guide him. Unfortunately, he was a wanted man and knew he would do some serious time if he surrendered. He believed he would get caught sooner than later, and when he did get arrested he promised God that he would read his Bible every day.

In 1999, I telephoned my dad in Texas and informed him I was getting married. I knew he was a wanted man, but I hoped he would come out to Oregon for my wedding. He arrived in Portland high on meth, which had been obtained from my sister, Star. Three nights later we were arrested for assault and my dad would spend the next several years in prison....

> *"Addictions are not about feeling good or getting high; they are about ways to be free of stress and pain, thus temporarily feeling normal...."*
> Michael Dye, Creator of The Genesis Process

personal reflection

The pain involved in the lives of my parents only escalated as they tried to find hope in themselves, other people, and substances. Looking back on their struggles, it is easy for me to see how they brought the pain of their pasts into each of their new relationships.

I often wonder why we never see that coming. Is it because we are so in love? Or is it the dopamine high from experiencing a new relationship? It was interesting to see much of the same dysfunction in our home when we became Christians. We attended church and lived for God, but ended up extremely broken. Could it be that church people struggle with the same issues as everyone else?

four

ON BROKEN ROAD

"And He who sat upon the throne said, 'Behold, I make all things new.'"
Revelation 21:5

After Mom divorced Hal, she went through a season of loneliness. She was depressed, alone, and spent days lying in bed. The pain of her failed relationships immobilized her. That is when she realized it was time to make real changes. That is when Jesus Christ (the forgiveness factor), began healing her heart. He brought back joy and hope. She was ready to risk everything in trusting God. She stopped dating and focused her energy on personal healing and self-care. She began taking classes at church on how to set boundaries. A lot of her time was spent in prayer and listening to God. Her healing grew as she increased her understanding of trauma and its impact on families.

She started being vulnerable and opening herself up to trust God. The Bible opened up to her like never before. The trust started with Jesus Christ, and in Him, she found life. She found forgiveness in Him and learned to forgive others. She remembers praying for God to send her a kinsmen redeemer. This is the biblical story of Ruth and Boaz from the Old Testament Book of Ruth. She put a picture on the wall of her house with two empty chairs sitting on a beach. She asked God to fill the chair of her heart with a man of God. She waited on God, knowing He would be faithful!

She grew in her identity as a child of God, and felt His love. As she grew in Him, she started attending the single's ministry at her church. She felt led to move beyond herself and build friendships. It was there that she met Gary. He was coming out of a season of failed relationships and addictive behavior. He also wanted to change and trust God with his life. Gary was gentle and loving in nature. Together, they attended country dance classes and soon began dating. They prayed together and talk for hours about God. As their dating became serious, they agreed on one very important fact: remaining pure and following God's guidelines for a blessed relationship. They both understood the pain and brokenness of doing things their own way. This commitment would eventually bless many generations. They became best friends.

It was not long after this that Gary asked mom to marry him. He knew she was the one for him. She wholeheartedly accepted, and they were married in 1997. They have been crazy for each other ever since.

Mom and Gary

Over the years their marriage has positively influenced all of us kids. We have seen the fruit of a marriage built upon the rock of Jesus. I am happy to say that they are still happily married today. They worship and pray together. The foundation of godly principles has helped them remain strong in their marriage. Sure, they have had their difficulties, but with God at the center, they have been victorious. Mom and Gary have been mentors to many people; they have taught classes on marriage and breaking the noose of the past. They are active in their church and cherished by their kids and grandchildren.

I appreciate Gary for being a man of his word and a model of commitment. He loves my mom as Christ loves the church. Meaning, he lays down his life for her, serves her, and values her over all worldly things. His love for God gives him the strength to love

Mom & Gary

my mom with honor and courage. Gary is a modern day knight who shines as he gives sacrificially to others.

Mom has been thriving in her role as his wife. She can trust him and knows that God is at the center of their marriage. With Gary's support, she has been able to work through the deeper wounds in her life. I love watching him patiently love her when she is having a difficult time. My mom has also had a significant healing effect on his life. Gary and Mom are not the same people I knew fourteen years ago; they are both transforming into the image of Christ. They are reconciling with their children and are a blessing to all of their grandchildren. The character of Christ is evident in both of their lives. It is simply amazing!

Grammy and her Princesses

prison set him free

When my dad went to jail in 1999, I personally believed it would be a continuation of his previous 30 years. There were quite a few of us that had written him off, but God had a different plan in mind. He continued to knock at the door of Dad's heart until he opened it for eternity. I guess some people have to see the inside of a prison cell multiple times before God can enter their heart. It was there, in his prison cell, that he was able to receive God's mercy and forgiveness.

When he arrived at the Multnomah County Jail, he was housed with a man named Henry who told him that God wanted him to read the Bible. They stayed up late into the night, as Henry taught my dad truths about God's word. Dad was transferred out the next day to another jail where he joined a Bible study. It was during the Bible study that my dad received Jesus Christ into his heart as Lord and Savior. This choice confirmed the fact that prayer works! Many people had prayed that he would give his life and heart to Jesus Christ. God is faithful to answer the prayers of His people.

In jail, he had another vision from God (remember he did not know much about the Bible at this time). The vision was of Jesus riding toward my fad on a white horse. When Jesus opened his mouth, out came a double-edged sword, turning into the Bible. On one side was the Old Testament and on the other side was the New Testament. Jesus said, "I have healed you, cleansed you, and chosen you." It pierced his heart. He called his second wife's husband, who was a Christian and elder in his church, and asked what it meant. He said, "You are a new creation, and Jesus has a plan for your life." From that point on, Dad has surrendered his life to his Lord and Savior Jesus Christ. That was 11 years ago. Shortly after receiving the Lord, a server in the jail gave him a Bible. Inside the cover it read:

To Anthony,
This is the book of life, not of religion. It is a love letter to you from God the Father, and our Savior of the whole earth the Lord Jesus Christ, written down through the ages by the Holy Spirit, through man. The Word of God in the Bible gives you a choice. Choose life or death, and the new life comes through Jesus Christ our Lord. He loves you unconditionally and we love you too.
Signed, The Jail People

He served three and a half years in prison, reading his Bible every day, and leading countless people/inmates to the Lord. God also put him alongside every person and ethnic group that he was prejudiced against. He sought forgiveness and relationship. God was doing a miraculous healing in his life. He was taken off the psychotropic meds and placed in the hands of God.

Upon his release from prison, he returned to Texas to be near my brother Chance, who was born with broken collarbones and was blind in the right eye. Dad felt led to pray for his son, and immediately Chance had his vision restored. Chance yelled, "I can see! I can see!" They experienced the miracle together. God continued to remind him to build the temple, and finally he understood what God meant: it was him, he was the temple that God wanted to build. He had every intention of staying in Texas and raising Chance, but Chance's mom was not open to following Jesus. My dad's friend was dying of cancer in Oregon, so he moved there. His friend was healed, and my dad eventually married the friend's daughter Kris. She also had a very difficult life and they chose to honor God in their lives through marriage. At the writing of this book, they've been married for six years. Their love represents the faithfulness of God.

It was not long before Dad was attending church and ministering at the Klamath County Jail. He was a natural with inmates because they can't say, "You don't understand what we are going

Dad & Kris

through." He does! Moreover, he just points them to Jesus every time. He has led many prisoners to the Lord. He also ministers to the youth at the juvenile home.

During this time, he was able to be with his dad during his last days on earth. God unleashed a great healing during their time together. This presented the opportunity for my dad to hold my grandfather in his arms as he passed into eternity. The officiating pastor of my grandfather's memorial service did a fantastic job honoring his life. My dad connected with him and began attending his church. As his leadership developed, God opened the door for Dad to become an elder. He is now an ordained minister and president of the Ambassador's for Christ jail ministry. God is good! Dad also felt the call to make amends for the trespasses of his past. He went to an old friend from whom he had stolen a gun and asked for forgiveness. He has sought reconciliation and asked forgiveness from those who are receptive.

One of the most powerful acts of God's healing came from asking for forgiveness from my mom's parents. Dad knew they feared him and had deep resentment for his past actions. He wrestled with how to approach them and spent much time in prayer before finally driving to their home. When my grandmother heard him knock on their door she motioned to my grandfather saying, "Johnny, the preacher is here," referring to their pastor. They did not know it was my dad. When my grandfather opened the door, he graciously invited him in. As Dad joined them in their living room, he began to weep and ask for their forgiveness. They were deeply moved by his repentant heart and forgave him. Then they all held hands as Dad prayed over their family. Please understand that my grandparents were not social people, and to have "this man" come in and pray with them is something that not even their pastor had done.

Dad is full of light and the darkness has faded. He loves his children and desires healing for their relationships. I have had an amazing reconciliation and friendship with him. Jesus Christ is the forgiveness factor that changed his life.

"Therefore, if anyone is in Christ,
the new creation has come:
The old has gone, the new is here!"
2 Corinthians 5:17

personal reflection

This chapter has been a lifetime in the making. Today I write as a son of two parents who follow Jesus Christ, the forgiveness factor that brought them out of shame, guilt, addictions, and broken relationships. He is the one who changes lives! On their own they could not change, but with Him everything changes. This is truth. This is all about God's redemptive power to wounded souls.

Not only do I have a new family today, but we also look forward to celebrating God's goodness throughout eternity. My children are blessed. My life will never be the same. God's love and compassion can touch even the darkest souls.

Dad's baptism by the Chaplain in 2000

Dad supervising
prison parolees

five

MY STORY: ROOTS

"The biggest disease today is not leprosy or tuberculosis, but rather the feeling of being unwanted."

Mother Teresa

In the previous four chapters you have read the life summary of my parents. Obviously, I could not include every detail, but I have given you a taste of who they were and who they have become in Christ Jesus. Now I will share my story.

My first memory of spending time with my father was flying a balsa wood plane in the front yard of my mom's home. I was living with her and her second husband, Bill. Dad had been released from prison (I didn't know this), and I was excited to see him.

Dad & me in 1975

I vividly remember twisting the propeller of the plane to tighten the rubber band as I floated it in his direction. I remember his smile and affectionate laugh. It seemed like that afternoon lasted a lifetime. In my eyes, he was my hero and I wanted to be just like him when I grew up. Our time together ended too soon. I knew in my heart that I loved him and he loved me.

My mom was a constant caregiver and loving influence in my life. I do not have a single memory of her lashing out or neglecting me as a child. My stepdad Bill was stern and authoritarian. I remember him chasing me with a tree switch on several occasions. I guess this was his way of implementing discipline (and I probably deserved it).

The most impactful memory I have of their few years together is of them having a violent argument in the bathroom of our home. Somehow, Mom's arm was cut because of a broken window. I remember sitting on the couch with my older stepbrother, scared to death and crying. I just didn't understand what was happening and why Mom was bleeding. Other than that event, it seemed like a normal situation. Our family did not go to church or have much of a social life.

Lori & Lisa

One of life's greatest blessings came from their relationship: my twin sisters Lisa and Lori. They were the most beautiful baby girls anyone had ever seen. Even though someone in the store asked, "Who is that little girl pushing the cart," I remember proudly pushing them through K-Mart as a little boy. I loved and cherished them. They were my little angels and friends.

When things turned sour for Mom and Bill, Mom moved my sisters and me into a trailer park. I distinctly remember black ants everywhere: in my bed, in our kitchen, all over everything. We stayed there for a couple months, eventually moving into a ranch style house.

I did not mind moving around, but felt extremely vulnerable and unprotected. I believe my mom and sisters felt this way, too. There were nights when we all slept in Mom's room with the door locked. I spent many fear-filled evenings sleeping in my closet or sneaking into my sisters' room to sleep under one of their beds. I was terrified of someone breaking into our house with the intent to hurt or kill us.

I found a sense of safety when I saw my dad during weekend visitations. He was remarried and living in a small town within a few miles of our house. I enjoyed hanging out with him and his wife. We did things like cut firewood, BBQ with their friends, and play in the woods. I sensed his wife truly loved me and she treated me as her own child. She became pregnant with my sister Star, five years younger than me. I loved her and enjoyed spending time with her. We were inseparables during our times together.

Star Bradley

fatherless

Despite only seeing my dad occasionally on the weekends, my life seemed normal. I thought everyone went through divorce and painful transitions. I didn't know what it felt like for a family to stay together. My mom had already been divorced twice and was working extremely hard to make our house a home. She was a waitress and often dropped us off at the YMCA before school. At times I felt like I was being raised by their staff. However, it was a positive environment for learning and building relationships. The YMCA had a great program promoting the growth and health of children. I was involved in classes, sports, swimming, and karate. I developed friendships with the other kids and staff. It was a fun place to be. I have great memories of the "Y."

Mom also signed me up for the Cub Scouts. We met at a neighbor's home and worked on earning our Scout badges. I never understood why men did not lead these groups. It was usually several women trying to teach boys how to become men. I often thought, "Where are all the dads?"

My two best friends were brothers who lived down the street with their divorced mom. We often spent the night with each other and rode our bikes around town. I have memories of their dad showing up drunk and breaking things in their house. I always wondered why most of my childhood friends had similar family backgrounds.

Mom began dating and had several boyfriends. I believe she did a good job of protecting my sisters and me from attaching to the first two, but one finally stuck around. His name was Randy, and he was the first adult male who treated me like a son. Yes, I would see my dad on visitations, but Randy was actively involved in my life. He built my first bicycle, took me to fly model rockets, and came to my soccer matches. I really loved him and knew that he loved me. I secretly longed for him to marry my mom and be my dad. They bought me a beautiful black German shepherd that I named Bear. He was my constant companion and friend. I loved coming home from school and playing for hours with him in the back yard. Bear's presence in our home provided some security for me. I know now that I was a deeply insecure little boy who longed for stability. Bear gave me a sense of ownership and worth.

it's my fault

Then one day, at the kitchen table in our home, I saw Mom crying. When I asked her what was wrong, she said, "Oh, nothing really." I said, "Mom, why are you crying?" She explained that Randy did not want to marry her. He did not want to settle down or raise a bunch of kids. I went into my room and wept. I thought Randy did not want to marry my mom because of me. I thought he did not want kids, and I was the source of his rejection.

I went outside to find comfort by playing with Bear, but he was gone! This broke my heart and I was enraged. I cried and thought, "How could he do this to me? How could Randy leave? Why would he take Bear? What is happening?" I was devastated.

Randy moved out and took my dog with him! I secretly cried for days. The two things I loved most in life had been taken from me. It took a while to process those feelings, and just when I seemed to forget, I saw Bear tied to a telephone pole just a few blocks away from our house. Randy had moved into a mobile home and kept my dog tied up outside. I approached Bear and started petting him, remaining there until Randy returned. When he arrived, he tried to explain what happened, but basically blew me off. It hurt knowing I wasn't treasured by him anymore. I made a vow that day: do not give your heart to another father figure. From that day forward, I believed I was on my own.

sexual abuse

It was during this time of my life that I was sexually abused. I sometimes spent time at my paternal grandparents' home. My two uncles and an aunt lived with them. One of my uncles was a known pedophile (I did not find this out until later in life). He began grooming me for sexual abuse. He was friendly, affirming, and encouraged me to drink alcohol and smoke pot with him. My first drink and marijuana high were at the age of seven. I remember getting extremely drunk on a couple different occasions; both times I blacked out.

In this environment, his inappropriate touching and oral sex began. The first time he touched me was in a tent outside my grandparents' house. Children were singing and playing in the yard next to theirs. It felt like time stood still. I knew it was wrong but I was afraid to say anything or confront him. He was an adult and I was supposed to be safe with him. He instructed me not tell anyone, especially my dad. This continued for several years.

I was also sexual abused by my babysitter, a family friend who lived down the street. It is interesting seeing how both acts of abuse began around the same time. My babysitter began grooming me for sexual experiences by letting me stay up later than my sisters and allowing me to watch R rated movies. I can remember, with great detail, my first experience with sexual intercourse. It was in our family room while I was playing Atari video games. I was eight years old. The abuse lasted two years. Again, I was told not to say anything. I learned to live two lives. One people knew of and loved; the other was lived in secrecy and isolation.

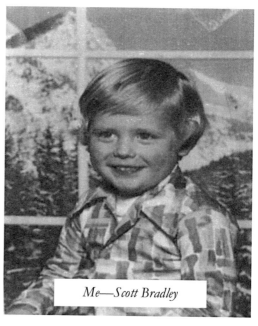

Me—Scott Bradley

Both perpetrators used secrecy and isolation to protect themselves. This solidified my belief that authority figures are absent of integrity and moral judgment. The abuse, and major father wounds, left me as a very troubled youth. I embraced secrecy as a way of life and survival. My identity was now formed around what I could offer people, not who I was as an individual. My innocence was stolen from me, and I was left carrying adult emotions and concerns.

troubles

I was suspended from elementary school on several occasions. One time I rubbed my teacher's head mimicking vulgarity that I learned from watching a Cheech and Chong movie. Another time I brought a box knife to school and threatened to stab a student. Interestingly enough, I was a great student and very intelligent, just lacking emotional stability and control.

In spite of the trouble I was getting into, I had an amazing second grade teacher. His name was Mr. Hodges; his influence still touches my heart. He invested in my life, took me to sporting events, and showed me the National Guard Armory. He was patient, affirming, and praised my mathematical abilities. I continue to thank God for placing him in my life.

transition

After Randy left, Mom started dating Hal. He had a rock band with his sons and they played at local bars and taverns. I enjoyed hanging out with them. I was excited to see my mom happy.

After my mom and Hal married, we started going to church. I did not really understand what was going on because I had never been to church before. I did not know what Jesus was all about, or what role God played in our lives. I began attending Royal Rangers (a ministry similar to Cub Scouts) meetings at the Assembly of God church. I loved the pine wood derby races. We played basketball and went on cool adventures. I felt that God was beginning to change our lives.

personal reflection

It is difficult to write out my story in such detail. I smile, reflecting on Mom's love, despite her failing relationships. I am pleased, knowing that Dad tried to have a relationship with me in the midst of his pain and addiction. I am not trying to sugarcoat the obvious difficulties, but I see them in a different light now. For years I struggled with the consequences of abuse, neglect from other caregivers, and father wound issues. I thought of myself as damaged goods. Shame and insecurity has been a constant companion in my life. Today I work hard to stay centered and focused on the truth of God's love for me.

six

ENTER SON OF MAN

"Forgiving means to pardon the unpardonable, faith means believing the unbelievable and hoping means to hope when things are hopeless."
G. K. Chesterton

My life forever changed the afternoon Hal shared the gospel with me. He told me that Jesus died for my sins, and that I could be in heaven with God if I asked Jesus into my heart. That day I asked Jesus to be my Lord and Savior. The following Sunday, I was baptized at Shasta Way Christian Church. At ten years old, I really loved Jesus and wanted Him to change my life. I found forgiveness in Christ and a new vision for my life.

I wanted to be like Hal. He was an amazing worship leader and preacher. After we moved to Selah, Washington, Hal was employed at a nursing home, and we moved to a house in the country. I loved going down to the river to play in the water with my sisters and our friends. Hal was preaching and leading worship in several churches. We also had a street ministry that helped care for prostitutes and their children. We served as a family, and the pain of my troubled past seemed far behind me.

One afternoon my mom was an emotional wreck. She was crying, saying she was going to leave Hal. She thought he was having an affair. He emphatically denied it. I did not understand what was happening, but I noticed that Hal was basically two different people. He appeared lively, charismatic, and relational at church. At home he seemed distant and unaffectionate. From my perspective, he did not show the same the love and affirmation to his family that he did to those at church.

the in crowd

Hal moved our family to Florence, Oregon. I enjoyed living in Florence, because the "in crowd" at my school quickly accepted me. It was not long before I forgot about the pain and loss of our friends in

Washington. Moving became easier as I learned to be a chameleon. I learned to fit in by being what people wanted. In Florence, the most popular kids became my closest friends, and I felt great. All of the external affirmation helped fill the hole in my heart. I played sports and got good grades. I loved hanging out at the beach in the warm sun with my sisters and friends. Summertime was great and I looked forward to staying there permanently. However, within a year, we moved again.

I did not receive the warm welcome in the small town of Mapleton that I had experienced in Florence. The other kids were bonded and did not accept outsiders. I felt alone and confused. I tried everything I could to fit in, even attempting to steal chewing tobacco from a store for one of the kids during a church-led excursion to Florence. I was busted for shoplifting and taken before the principal. He tried to explain that I did not need to "steal" to get the approval of other kids. I was ashamed that I was caught. About the time things started getting comfortable, we moved again. This time it was halfway across the state to Lebanon.

During our travels, I rarely visited my dad. I heard he had remarried and was living in Chiloquin. His third wife had a daughter and they seemed to be happy. He owned a logging truck company, and he even let me drive his log truck down a country road. However, I did not know all the details surrounding his life.

I had a hard time adjusting in Lebanon. I found a crowd that liked to drink and fight. We also smoked a lot of pot. I grew detached from my mom and family. After living in Lebanon for about a year, Hal decided to start a church in a local abandoned theater. He led worship and did most of the preaching and pastoral care. My mom helped with the children. The church began to grow. During this time, I continued to rebel. I started binge drinking and having sex with multiple partners. I was caught stealing hundreds of dollars in cash from a local thrift store. I was living two different lives: church boy on Sundays and rebellious outlaw the rest of the week. This double life started to take its toll. My grades began to fall and my life was a wreck. Mom and my stepdad did not know what to do with me.

I went to visit Dad in the summer of 1989 after he moved back to Klamath Falls. He lived alone in an apartment, and I really enjoyed the freedom this presented me. He asked if I wanted to come live with him. I did not really know him or anything about his lifestyle; I just knew I just wanted to be with my hero. Besides, the whole church thing was a joke, and I needed to become a man. Mom did not want me to go. However, after I threw a huge fit and told her that I hated her, she let me go.

I moved in with Dad, registered for high school, and re-connected with my childhood friends, including the same best friends from elementary school. Living with my dad presented a level of freedom that I desperately desired. I wanted to be an adult and prove myself trustworthy.

Dad sat me down one day and said, "Son I'm going to give you enough rope to hang yourself." It did not take long before I would do just that! I started partying hard with my old buddies and using drugs. I had multiple girlfriends and countless sexual relationships. Wild parties at my house included drinking and fighting. I was barely making it to school and close to dropping out. On several occasions Dad and I drank and smoked pot together.

infidelity

While I was living in Klamath Falls, my mom found out that my stepdad Hal had been sleeping around. They had to resign from leading their church and were publically humiliated. My mom and sisters were traumatized. Mom and Hal moved to Gresham, Oregon, near Portland. There they discovered a church that offered healing and support for Hal's sexual addiction. The pastor was famous for helping pastors with infidelity and sexual addictions. Hal found work at a nursing home and helped with the worship team at church.

I started getting into a lot of trouble in Klamath Falls. I acquired several minor in possession of alcohol and disorderly conduct charges, which led to time in and out of the juvenile home. I was also busted for drinking and fighting at school. This led to my first drug and alcohol rehabilitation stay. It was a 90-day program, and I made it two weeks before leaving, breaking my probation. Once I was arrested, I spent several weeks in the juvenile home, and then was put back on probation. I was ordered to return to rehab, but never made it back.

expelled

I entered my senior year of high school a serious troublemaker. The principal scheduled a meeting with my dad (he never made it) to set very clear guidelines for my participation. I had to walk the line; nothing outside of excellence would be tolerated. I made it three weeks before I was expelled for drinking and fighting at a football game. I broke a skater's arm with his own skateboard. This brought assault charges, which violated my probation. After spending several weeks incarcerated at the juvenile home, I was released to stand trial at a later date. After this incident, my destructive behavior increased.

Dad got me a job working at the local motorcycle shop dismantling Harleys. His friend who owned the shop was one of Klamath's biggest druggies. Dad hoped I would discover a talent working on bikes. That job lasted about a month. I started drinking and doing drugs daily. I knew I would not go back to high school, and submitted to the fact that my life would be one institution after another. I thought it was just a matter of time until I would be serving a serious sentence in jail or prison.

I did not call or see my mom much. I was ashamed of what I had become. Running from my pain seemed like the best option to feel normal. In my state of self-rejection, I believed my only options were dealing drugs or doing time. I lost hope and thought that I had made too many mistakes. I was in the system, and "the man" was obviously out to get me.

One of the things that earned me respect and credibility was fighting, so I started fighting all the time. It did not matter who or where. If there was a fight, I seemed to be involved. There were drunken brawls with Native Americans almost every weekend. Several of my friends were killed living this chaotic lifestyle. The pain of losing my friends only added to my shame and self-rejection. I did not know how to grieve or process my feelings. I believed my only option was to medicate the pain through anger, substance abuse, and sexual highs.

One afternoon in the spring of 1991, two groups of young men got involved in a drunken brawl. It was similar to seeing two gangs fighting in the street of a large city. I was the ringleader of one group and called out the ringleader of the other group. We started the fight in the yard, which escalated onto the driveway. I repeatedly kicked and hit him. When he fell, I continued booting him. Finally, one of my friends pulled me back because the young man quit moving. He was covered in blood and barely breathing. I panicked and left running, along with a group of my friends.

Once we heard the sirens from the fire trucks, ambulances, and police, we went to a friend's house to hide. I was terrified. I thought I had killed him and did not know what to do. This was not exciting anymore, it was serious. I was in big trouble. The owner of the house convinced me to turn myself in, claiming self-defense.

I went back to the scene and was arrested for first-degree assault. They took me directly to the juvenile home. I was seventeen years old.

Me in high school

I knew I would be incarcerated for a while because my dad was down in Reno partying with his crew. I was hoping he would find out what happened and bail me out. However, the court set no bail, and I was looking at three to four years in prison, if remanded to the adult court system. I sat in my cell wondering how I could've done such a horrible thing. What was I going to do?

The young man did not die, but was seriously injured. He wanted to press charges, and I was ready to take responsibility. I did not have any money, so I was given a court appointed attorney. My attorney said I should try to make a deal for 18 months in prison. When Dad found out about this, he hired an attorney for me, someone he knew well—the attorney who sent him to prison for manslaughter 20 years prior. My dad trusted his counsel and felt comfortable paying for his services. As I sat in the juvenile home, they worked out a deal with the prosecutor. I would get credit for time served and spend my next three months in the county jail.

I was a seventeen-year-old pretty boy, placed in the "C Pod" of the Klamath County Jail. The "C Pod" housed inmates with the harshest punishments—long-term county sentences or headed to prison. Most were Native Americans and related to each other. I had already made a few enemies among this group. I was terrified, but I could not show it. I spent my eighteenth birthday alone in my cell, wondering what had happened to my life. Where would I go from here? What did this world have to offer me? I was so consumed with my personal misery that I never once asked God to set me free. I hated who I had become, and felt great remorse for the pain I was causing others. The harder I tried to change myself, the further I felt from God. What I know now is that only Jesus can change us from the inside out.

I was released from jail in June 1991. The officers led me out the gate and wished me good luck. No one was waiting for me and no one seemed to care that I existed. Once again, I was alone, trying to figure out what to do with my life. Where would I turn from here?

personal reflection

To survive in life, I learned to be a master chameleon. If people worshipped God, I worshipped God. If people drank whiskey, I drank whiskey. If people snorted coke, I snorted coke. My greatest desire was to be accepted. I believe my desire for acceptance began during the transitions of life.

My mastery of chameleonolgy (I just made that word up) happened as we moved around as a family. I knew how to fit in at any cost. I felt valued through acceptance, even if it meant I was going against my conscience. I acted like a chameleon all through school and into adulthood. This deep desire for acceptance can take on a life of its own. In recovery/counseling language, this is called a protective personality, which is created to keep us from trusting others, being vulnerable, and from being betrayed and hurt. Pride is another form of protection. Pride helped me push others away, communicating "I do not need you." Pride helped me feel powerful and unsafe to others, and that was how I liked it. Isolated and alone, so no one could hurt me again. This persona kept me from the very thing that would help me—a vulnerable, trusting relationship with God and other safe people.

This led to increased addictive behavior, or what the Bible calls bondage. Our basic needs are not met, and we begin to die inside. The addictive mind lacks self-esteem, self-respect, humility, and self-concern. As addicts, we live in an ambivalent state. It is an oxymoron, that people can serve themselves and hate themselves at the same time.

The truth is that wounded people believe they literally are their "sin." They miss the fact that God gives them their identity. Instead of knowing who they are, they believe "they are what they do." This lie keeps people trapped for years.

seven

RELEASED INTO BONDAGE

"One who was there had been an invalid for thirty-eight years. When Jesus saw him lying there and learned that he had been in this condition for a long time, he asked him, "Do you want to get well?"
John 5:5-7

As I walked out of the door of the jail, I walked right back into my old behaviors. I felt abandoned because no one was there to pick me up, which led to me say, "Forget it, I can't trust anyone. Where are all my so-called friends and family?" Once again, I vowed to trust no one. I called a friend to pick me up and proceeded to get blacked-out drunk. I missed being with my friends and I missed the temporary numbness that comes from binge drinking. I got drunk, knowing my probation strictly prohibited drinking. The consequence of breaking my probation: 36 to 48 months in prison.

At some point during the evening, I found a ride back to my dad's house. He woke up and discovered me passed out beside one of his cars. He kicked me several times to wake me, and was extremely angry that I would do this "after all he had done to keep me from going to prison." I was still drunk, and he demanded I leave his property. He did not want to see my "miserable face" again. I grabbed my coat and stumbled down the street trying to figure out how I ended up in his yard, just a day after being released from jail.

I decided to call one of my friends. We pooled together our money and headed for Crater Lake, where we spent three weeks camping in the woods and buying beer at the lodge. We met a couple girls who worked at the lodge and had a good time "blowing off some steam."

When we finally ran out of money, my friend said he needed to get back to Klamath. I knew I could not go back because there was nothing there for me. I decided to call my mom and see if she would take me in. She agreed to give me gas money if my friend would drive me to her place. I arrived in Gresham, Oregon, in the summer of 1991, excited to start a new life and make real changes.

summer job

Mom and Hal were still trying to resolve their issues through counseling and church work. They let me set up a room in their garage and helped me find a job. I finally landed a job as a salesman at a western wear store. Remember, I am good at becoming like the people around me. While living in Klamath Falls, I became a total redneck, so I fit in well with this crowd.

Things were going well, and I had my probation transferred to Portland. Like so many times before, I started drinking and partying with people from work. They were the typical "urban cowboy" crowd who liked to have a good time. I became good friends with a Warm Springs Native American and we often hung-out after work. I enjoyed his conversation and sense of humor. He also worked at the western wear store.

The company announced an employee party and celebration at the owner's home. I was excited to attend and possibly find a new girlfriend. Everyone had a great time eating BBQ, drinking alcohol, and playing volleyball. As the party was winding down, one of the owner's friends asked me if I wanted to take the party to nearby Vancouver, Washington. I was in. He said I could ride with him and we would find a bar to hang out at. I explained to him that I was only eighteen and he said that was not a problem. He was approximately 35 to 40 years old. I did not know his real name, since people just called him Cowboy. We tried to enter a couple bars, but I was carded each time. He invited me to have a beer at his place, and I thought this was a great idea.

As we were pulling out of the last bar, he saw a woman walking down the road and said, "Let's see if she wants to party with us." As he drove back around, she was gone. Then he grew angry and whispered, "We could've raped her." I thought that was very strange, but kept my mouth shut. This guy was obviously disturbed and possibly very dangerous. But I played it "cool" and we went back to his apartment. Upon arriving, we drank a beer, and he told me I could sleep on the floor of his guest room. He threw a blanket on the floor, and I turned in for the night.

Just as I began to fall asleep, I awoke to him trying to rape me. As I tried to wrestle away and get up, I kept falling to the ground. I was enraged and terrified at the same time. He kept grabbing at me and finally tackled me. His breathing was loud and he forcefully said, "Calm down. Calm down. It'll be okay." I immediately broke loose and slammed him into the wall. I proceeded to beat him and told him if he got up, I would really mess him up. When he agreed to stay put, I grabbed my stuff, and took off down the street. I did not know where I was, what time it was, or his real name. I found a pay phone and called a cab. I arrived back in Gresham at four in the morning. When I went back to work, I tried to tell the owners what happened and they just laughed it off. "What? Cowboy? Come on, he's just a little guy. You guys were just drunk. He was probably just messing with you," they said. I didn't push it. This was a very traumatic event in my life because it brought back many memories of childhood sexual abuse.

Shortly after this incident, I tried to join the Marines. I met with a local recruiter and he did a background check. Because of my past criminal offenses, I was rejected. I did not know what to do at this point. I wanted to make a new start, but even the Marines wouldn't take someone like me.

I began to develop a friendship with my mom's next-door neighbor, a devout Christian named Julie. She took me to church and encouraged me to go back to high school. She was finishing her senior year and invited me to join her. After contemplating this for a while, I agreed to try school one more time. I did not know if they would even let me register because of my history. However, to my surprise, they allowed me to return, and I was scheduled to graduate in the summer of 1992. I believe that God was gently knocking on the door of my heart through my friendship with Julie. He was whispering, "Son, I love you. You can come home now." But I wasn't ready to listen yet.

When I returned to the classroom I didn't know what to expect. The only person I knew was Julie. I started out as kind of a loner, but people were welcoming. Each day was refreshing, and I developed a great relationship with several staff members. I did well in school, and was eventually voted "Mr. Sam Barlow" for the 1991/92 school year.

The election came in the form of a generic talent contest. The contest included several categories: swim suit, talent, speech. During my talent portion I lip-synced Garth Brooks' song, *If Tomorrow Never Comes*. I walked down into the crowd and handed my mom a rose. Taking her hand in mine, I brought her onstage. There was not a dry eye in the room. I guess that sealed the win for me, but it also allowed me to honor my mom.

During one of my trips to Julie's youth group, I was introduced to Ken, who eventually became my best friend. We had similar pasts. The night I met him, we looked at each other from across the pew, and he said, "Let's go get drunk." I said, "Sounds good." That began a long-term friendship that would last many years. We started hanging out all the time. He was a couple years older than me and had a car. He would pick me up from school or my mom's house and we would go party. We drove around with a keg in the backseat of his car, filling our cups and looking for trouble. I got into a few fights but they never involved the law. Until one night, we went to a party with some of my friends from high school. Ken drove several of us to the party and we proceeded to get drunk. On the way home, he drove off the road, and we crashed into a couple trees. I was knocked unconscious and had to be dragged up to the road. When I woke up, I was extremely upset with Ken.

The party host found us and offered a ride to my place. As I got out of their car, Ken punched me in the back of the head. I proceeded to rough him up a little. He left stumbling down the street. The police picked him up and brought him back to my house. The officers questioned my entire family as to what had happened. I told them it was self-defense, and was not charged with a crime. I told Ken not to come around ever again. I believed he was trying to get me thrown into prison since I was still on probation.

Without my best friend in my life, I started searching for new friendships. This continued until the spring of 1992, when I started dating a girl from school. I fell head over heels in love with her. Even though I had been with many girls before, she was the first girl I truly loved. She was a cheerleader and came from a Christian home. Her parents did not approve of me, but they tolerated me. I spent all my time with her and we made plans to go to college together. My drinking had slowed down, but I did get drunk on several occasions, and that bothered her. She became concerned when I was arrested on another MIP (minor in possession) charge during spring break.

I was terrified that my probation officer would learn about the MIP, so I quit checking in. He put a warrant out for my arrest. I was now living a life of anxiety and fear. If they ever caught up with me, I knew I would be sent to prison. My girlfriend convinced me to go see my probation officer so we could move on with our lives. When I arrived at his office, another officer came from behind, slammed me face down on the desk, slapped handcuffs on me, and read me my rights. I was detained at the Multnomah County jail. Fortunately, my girlfriend's father posted bail while I waited for a court hearing to determine my future. I begged my probation officer to give me another chance. I told him about my plans to finish high school and go to college. I was given another chance and my girlfriend was by my side.

I graduated from high school in June 1992, ready to start a new life. My girlfriend and I decided to go to college in Albany, Oregon, since her sister was attending Oregon State University in nearby Corvallis. We planned to live with her sister until we could find our own place. I worked all summer, and my mom helped me purchase a car.

We both registered for classes at Linn Benton Community College and started completing our courses. I enjoyed going to school and working at the local feed store. On our second trip home to Gresham, I found out that Hal had left my mom for another woman. Both Mom and my twin sisters looked miserable. It came as a surprise to me because I thought they were doing well. I was deeply troubled by this, but could not do anything about it. I believed my girlfriend loved me unconditionally, but I had an undercurrent of pain and shame that would not leave my life. I started partying again and was thrown in jail for disorderly conduct. Fortunately, I was in another county and my probation was not violated. (It should've been a hundred times!) My girlfriend started complaining because I drank too much. I told her I would slow down on the drinking, but my partying continued.

I ran into a couple of old school friends who also liked to party, so I spent a lot of time with them. We started drinking and doing meth for days at a time. I finally told my girlfriend that it was over and she needed to move on. Several times she came looking for me, but I constantly denied my love for her.

The problem was, I did love her, but when I was sober I was depressed and suicidal. That is when my drug use progressed into a daily habit. I started buying and selling crank to support my addiction. The drinking, drugs, and women kept me from thinking about all my problems. I drove to Portland to party and see my family.

After I re-connected with Ken and moved back to Portland, I started using cocaine, meth, and pills. This downward spiral led to me to being homeless and living off 82nd Avenue, a hub of drugs and prostitution in Portland. I fell into a pattern of using everyone and anything I could get my hands on. I was involved with prostitutes and drug trafficking that included dealing, using, and slamming cocaine. Outrageous parties lasted for days; I was involved in orgies and finally started having sex in exchange for drugs. I was literally hopeless and searching for a way to die. I hated myself and all that I was doing. It was a very dark season of life. I knew people cared for me, but I did not care about myself. No one could stop this crazy train. The remarkable thing is that I was never arrested for using or trafficking drugs. When I finally burned all my bridges, I decided to leave Portland.

personal reflection

I have read and re-read this chapter about this season of my life a hundred times. I still don't know how I couldn't "wake up and smell the coffee." What was I thinking? Was I thinking at all? My life was a roller coaster ride from hell, going to college one day and living like a homeless dope fiend the next. Does that make sense to you? It doesn't to me. Addiction doesn't make sense. People who carry promise and potential can be lured into the dark caverns of addiction.

"Pain is God's megaphone to a deaf world."
CS Lewis

eight
ON THE RUN

"Forgiveness is giving up the possibility of a better past."
Unknown

I moved back to Corvallis and stayed with trusted friends. We partied frequently and I eventually quit contacting my probation officer. This was the same probation that I received three years prior. If I was arrested, I knew I would do prison time. One evening my friend and I drove to Portland to party with some friends. I proceeded to get drunk and then tried driving back to Corvallis. I began falling asleep at the wheel, so I stopped at a rest area. I woke up with four police cruisers surrounding my vehicle and an officer beating on my driver side window demanding I come out with my hands in the air. They ran my plates and did a background check on the owner of the vehicle.

As I tried to figure out what was going on, the officers ripped the door open. They threw me to the ground and handcuffed my arms behind my back. There was a warrant out for my arrest in Klamath County. I was taken to the Multnomah County Jail in Portland, to be transferred back to Klamath County to face the same judge that previously sentenced me.

After a couple days in the Multnomah County Jail, several other inmates and I were placed on a prison bus. I clearly remember the driver and guards playing the song, *"Bad Boys, Bad Boys, Whatcha Gonna Do, Whatcha Gonna Do, When They Come for You"* during the whole trip. I guess it was supposed to be funny. The journey to the Klamath County Jail took five days. When I arrived a court date was set to discuss the violation of my probation and I was released. My friends picked me up in their motor home. We freebased coke on our way back to Portland, smoking it through the night and into the next week.

When I arrived back in Portland and told Mom what happened she was deeply troubled by my condition. She tried to help by giving me a place to stay. I kept my "nose clean" for a few weeks until my court appearance. Mom drove me to my court hearing in Klamath Falls. Ken joined us for what we thought would be a long goodbye. When we arrived at the courthouse, I spoke with my attorney who told me that the judge was still contemplating my sentence, and recommended that I plead for my life and give a concrete plan of action. I stood before the judge, asked her to show me mercy, and told her that I was truly a good person. She decided to give me another chance and let me off with an extended period of probation.

chronic

After returning to Portland, I became restless and went back to Corvallis. While staying with friends, I became interested in another young woman I knew from college. We were friends at school but never connected intimately. We ran into each other at a couple parties and began dating. She was a very sweet girl who loved her horses. Actually, her life was all about training and showing horses. I appreciated her genuineness and capacity to love others.

Within a few weeks, I was ready to get serious with her. However, there was something holding her back. Maybe she realized that I was trouble, or maybe she had strong boundaries. I don't know, but I won her heart and moved in with her. She lived on a 10-acre farm and had a couple other friends living with her. I wasn't aware that she actually owned her place, with her finances under the care of a trust fund. She finally opened up to me about her mother's death and the horrible circumstances that followed. Her mom had passed away from toxic shock poisoning and died a slow, agonizing death. Her family sued the feminine hygiene company responsible, and she received a large settlement. I didn't know how to process this and was not much support in her grief.

We continued to live together and she helped me become a horseman. I loved horses and began learning how to ride and rope. It did not take long before we were roping in rodeos and local events. I became obsessed with roping and the rush from competition. I felt I had finally found my identity as a real cowboy. I also learned how to shoe horses while traveling with other farriers. The men who taught me the trade became close friends.

My rodeo days

My girlfriend's heart was soft, and she supported me in every effort. This still did not stop my chronic partying and womanizing. I often spent weekends away at rodeos, drinking and sleeping around. I knew I had a good thing going with her and didn't want to break her heart. I did love her, but I could not love myself. There were many late night parties and brawls. I started using drugs again and visiting my friends in Portland. I lost interest in becoming a good man and focused entirely on partying. My girlfriend was ready to give me the boot and call off our relationship.

After another weekend of partying at rodeos and feeling horrible, I came clean about my secret behavior, and she asked me to leave. Attempting to change my ways, I checked myself into a rehab center located in Corvallis, Oregon. My girlfriend came to visit me a couple times, but at that point, I knew it was over.

While in rehab, Mom came to visit. She brought her new boyfriend Gary along. I respected his genuineness and soft-spoken nature. I didn't know he would become the husband that she truly desired. He was a man who loved her as Christ loves His church.

During one of my counseling sessions Mom joined us. I opened up about the sexual abuse from my childhood. I felt it was time that someone knew what I had experienced. I never told anyone about the abuse. I felt I was somehow responsible for it. Mom had no idea that her baby boy had experienced these things. We both wept, and connected at a level I had never experienced. Then she opened up about her experience with abuse as a child. I had no idea that she had wounds similar to mine. That was the first time I felt truly close to my mom. A deep level of trust developed and has not been broken since.

While in rehab, I completed my probation. I felt proud. I no longer had a prison sentence sitting over my head. After completing the rehab program, I started living with a friend near Monmouth, Oregon, and began dating a woman with a young daughter. Both of them loved me and wanted a future together. I wasn't ready for a commitment of this nature. I broke their hearts with my inconsistent behavior. My prayer is that the little girl doesn't carry the pain of my poor choices in her soul. I had no intention of hurting them. When I think of them, I am reminded of the pain I felt when Randy left us.

During this time I began working as a satellite dish technician for a cable television company. I didn't stay sober long and went right back to drinking. I stayed away from the drugs and felt like I was doing better. After losing my job, I decided to move to Bend, Oregon, with a family I knew. I worked at a factory where manufactured homes were built. My family friend and I continued to rodeo on the weekends and life was good. I started dating another girl I met in Monmouth, and she moved to Bend. We lived on a ranch near Redmond, Oregon, for about six months. I grew tired of my commitment to my girlfriend and asked her to move out. She moved to Snohomish, Washington. I needed some space to continue partying and running around with women. I stayed in Bend and lost my job at the factory.

While visiting my family in Portland, Mom asked me to come and listen to her speak during a church service. I did not know what to expect, but agreed to listen. The pastor, Dr. Ted Roberts, was giving a message on the grace of God and His power to heal the brokenhearted. Ted spoke in a way that made sense to me. He said he had been raised by seven stepfathers and struggled with addiction. He spoke of God becoming our father and that people do change. I was inspired and felt a connection with him. At the end of the message, Mom joined him on stage and shared her testimony. She began by telling her story and then shared about the transformation happening in her life. I wept as she spoke about forgiveness and the love of God. She explained how, for years, she prayed for my dad and me. She wept as she shared about her love for Jesus. I couldn't believe what I was hearing. My mom was a changed person! She was amazing. My heart was touched and I respected her journey. I also noticed Gary was right by her side to support and encourage her. They seemed to truly love each other, and I could tell love and respect was at the center of their relationship. I left that day with a glimmer of hope.

the postman

About that time, Kevin Costner was filming a movie nearby, and they were looking for extras. The extras were required to have horses, so my friend and I signed up. We got the job and spent two months filming the (epic) movie, *The Postman*. It was a great experience and an amazing adventure. We hung out with Kevin and the other actors. When hey moved the filming to the state of Washington near the Canadian border, my friend and I were asked by the producers to join them for six weeks. There was plenty of drinking and womanizing on set. I was involved with instigating a huge brawl between the cowboys and "hippies" that were filming another project. A Volkswagen bus was destroyed, and we were almost kicked off the film.

A couple weeks after we finished filming, I drove back to Portland to attend a wedding for Mom and Gary. I was so happy for them. I knew it was the real deal and I fully supported it. Mom was beautiful in her wedding gown. Gary looked handsome. I thought he resembled Robert Redford.

I stayed in contact with my girlfriend who had moved to Snohomish and we decided to reconcile. The only problem—I was living in Central Oregon and she was living in Northern Washington. I applied for several jobs in Washington and was hired by General Telephone. In the summer of 1997 I moved into a place with her and began working. We started out strong. We roped and made friends who were also horse people. I enjoyed working at the phone company and soon discovered I could make a career of it. The company invested in its employees, offering retirement, benefits, and company vehicles. It was my first opportunity to have a career and stable future. I felt blessed to receive this opportunity.

Nevertheless, as things always went, I continued to drink. I told my girlfriend I wanted to end our relationship, and we went back and forth for about a month. The breaking point came one evening when I arrived home from a local tavern, drunk. She met me on the porch and told me I needed to change. I did not like the fact that she was up in my "grill" and told her to get out of my face. She kept coming at me, pushing me up against the wall. That is when I lost my mind and ran inside to call 911. I told the dispatcher to send the police because I needed protection from my crazy girlfriend. They sent a sheriff and two deputies. In the meantime, her brother and friend were trying to calm me down. They separated us, and her brother's friend took me outside to speak some sense into me.

Filming "The Postman" with Kevin Costner

After repeated attempts to get me to listen, he confronted me. I proceeded to beat him down in my driveway and repeatedly slammed his head into the side of my vehicle. It left multiple dents in the door. That's when I heard the police cruisers coming up our driveway. I went back into the house, afraid they were going to question the guy I just beat up. For some odd reason, he never told the police what happened. When the officers arrived, they came to our front porch. My dog, a blue heeler, was all over them, not letting them near the door. I opened the door and called the dog in. They seemed irritated because the dog was extremely aggressive. I quickly informed them that everything was "cool" and they could take off. But the sheriff asked to come in and check things out. Reluctantly, I let them in, fearing that my girlfriend would say something to get me arrested, or tell them that I beat up her friend.

My emotions escalated and the officer told me to calm down. That infuriated me even further and I continued to raise my voice. That's when he grabbed my arm and attempted to restrain me. In a matter of seconds, I grabbed him and his partner, and threw them onto the floor of my living room. I slammed them to the ground, securing them both in my arms. When I realized what I had done, I let them loose and rolled back towards the couch. They reacted violently to my actions, dousing me with mace, ripping the shirt off my back, tie-wrapping my hands and feet, and dragging me to their car. I was arrested for assaulting two police officers. They took me to the Snohomish County Jail. As I sat in my cell, the same old questions kept running through my mind: How could I mess up my life again? What was I thinking? I had a great career and future; now I would lose everything. I was terrified and wept through the night.

The next morning I called my girlfriend and asked her to call my supervisor. I knew I made a major mistake and did not want to lose my job. She reluctantly called him and told him I was sick. I sat in jail through the weekend and the judge released me, pending a bond. After my girlfriend pulled a few thousand dollars together, I was released.

When I went back to work on Monday I knew I was in big trouble. I moved out of our place and began living with a friend from work. I hired a top-notch attorney, hoping he could get my charges reduced. I did not want to go to prison and especially didn't want to lose my job. It took him six months to reach a deal with the prosecutor. I would serve several months in the county jail, but I was also allowed to participate in a work release program. The court recognized that I had a career and gave me a chance to prove I could be true to my commitments. During the six months between the arrest and plea deal, I drank and ran around with women. I became involved with an older woman until I realized she was as dysfunctional as I was. We brought out the worst in each other and it ended quickly.

I served my sentence in the summer of 1998. I lived at the jail and went to work during the day. They monitored every job and every hour of my day. I hated living at the jail and quit eating healthy food. I only ate sunflower seeds and M&Ms. I did not talk to any of the other inmates and lost 30 pounds. I didn't believe I belonged there and did not want to make any friends. I would do my time and move on in life. And that's exactly what I did. I was released and went to live with a friend. It wasn't long before, guess what, I started drinking and using cocaine again. It got so bad that I started staying up for days at a time. The interesting thing is, I kept my job and actually excelled as an employee. I was living a double life. Even though I seemed to have things under control, I knew it was just a matter of time before I would lose it all. I felt destined to fail. I did not like who I had become and was carrying around a lot of baggage from my past.

personal reflection

I always felt comfortable in the eye of the storm. It helped me focus on external issues and not the heart issues that created my true pain. The constant crisis and addiction were anesthetics to the real issues in my life. I hated myself and never felt valuable. I had no hope or future. I knew my misery would end up killing me or someone else. The compass in my brain was pointing nowhere, but God's plan was a different course.

> *"For I know the plans I have for you,' declares the LORD, 'plans to prosper you and not to harm you, plans to give you hope and a future."*
>
> Jeremiah 29:11

nine

LONG DISTANCE ROMANCE

"If we confess our sins, he is faithful and just and will forgive us our sins and purify us from all unrighteousness."

1 John 1:9

I decided to visit my mom and twin sisters for Thanksgiving 1998. They were living in Gresham, Oregon. My sister Lisa had been telling me about a nice Christian girl from her salon that "I should really go out with." Since I had met Gwenna Davis a couple times and thought she was very nice, I was intrigued, but wasn't interested in a long-distance relationship. I did plan to arrive in Gresham on Wednesday evening so we could have dinner together.

Being the day before Thanksgiving, traffic between the Seattle area and Gresham was horrendous. I arrived at the restaurant fashionably late and was surprised to find all of them drinking and dancing. They had already eaten dinner and didn't wait for me to get the party started. We danced the night away and I enjoyed hanging out with Gwenna. On top of that, she was gorgeous! When we all gathered the next day for Thanksgiving dinner, I asked Gwenna if she would consider going on a date with me. She told me she already had plans with her ex-boyfriend. She explained that she was ending her relationship with him, and I could take her on a date some other time. I thought she was a strong and courageous woman. She had her own career, lived in her own apartment, and seemed close with her family. I thought she was a "keeper."

We agreed to start seeing each other as friends on the weekends. I made the three-and-a-half hour drive to Gresham almost every weekend. After a few weeks, we agreed to stay mutually committed to each other. This meant I would have to break off several connections I had, and she would do the same. We agreed to take it slow and see how things progressed. I had never done that before and was anxious about the commitment. I did not know how to settle down, not to mention keep my mind and eyes focused on one woman. I knew this was a once in a lifetime opportunity. Therefore, I stopped sleeping around and stayed true to her physically. Unfortunately, I still struggled with porn and other addictions.

Finally, in January of 1999, I convinced her to move to Seattle. I rented her an apartment and helped her re-locate. She found a job at a local salon, and we spent every moment together. We attended a couple of churches while in Seattle, but nothing really drew me in. She wanted to be part of a local church and it weighed heavy on her heart. I hadn't been to church much, but somewhere inside my heart, I knew God was doing a work in my life. I agreed to attend church, but that was pretty much it.

Gwenna

In the spring of 1999, I asked Gwenna to marry me. She agreed and we set a date in August. I sought a job transfer to Oregon; everything fell into place. I actually received a better job through the transfer. While in Seattle, we had purchased a dog and named him Romeo. He was the nervous puppy hiding in the corner of the breeder's house. I felt an instant connection with him and wanted to take him home. He became our first son and we loved him very much.

Romeo

Shortly before our wedding date we moved back to Gresham. I stayed with my best friend Ken and she stayed with her parents. In the time leading up to our wedding, I attended church with her family. They were extremely religious, with four generations sitting in the same aisle. I was a bit disturbed by this because I wasn't familiar with the concept of families staying together. I was used to chronic dysfunction and divorce, not commitment and stability. Nevertheless, I believed that they approved of me and thought I could become the man who would care for their daughter. They had no idea of the baggage I was bringing into their family.

Then there was my dad. I hadn't spoken to him in years, and I knew he was on the run, living in Texas. I was able to reach him by telephone and asked him to come to my wedding. He said he would do his best to make it and arrived two weeks later. I was so excited to see him and introduce my soon-to-be bride to my hero. We went to meet him at his hotel. Gwenna was a bit nervous, as she wanted to make a good impression. The moment he opened the door, I could tell he was high on crank and obviously delusional. He grabbed me, tackled me onto one of the beds, and tried to roughhouse.

Appalled by his behavior, Gwenna was speechless at his crude comments. On the way home I tried to explain that he was a dope fiend and asked her not to get too worried. She was concerned that he might make a scene at our wedding or do something crazy.

bachelor party

With all the wedding plans set, it was time for my bachelor party. With the help of Ken, I was able to contact most of my friends, and approximately 25 of them, mostly the cowboy type, showed up on a Thursday afternoon. I was to be married on the following Saturday morning. Ken lined up a large motor home for us to use for the evening. We started out drinking at his place then ventured out to several strip clubs and bars. At approximately ten in the evening, we took our drunken group to our final stop. This stop would change our lives forever.

It was a club full of female dancers with mostly men as patrons. I asked Dad to take a picture of some friends and me. The head bouncer grabbed the camera and said no pictures were allowed inside. I told him to chill out and let us have some bachelor party pictures. He proceeded to get in my face and told me if I did not listen, we would have to leave. I continued to argue with him until he finally grabbed my throat. He was going to physically remove me from the club. Then I heard my dad yell, "Don't touch my son," as he proceeded to punch the bouncer.

The place became a huge barroom brawl. Bar stools were flying, people were fleeing, and the women were screaming. The confrontation moved outside and continued to grow until the police arrived and took control of the situation. The officers placed my dad, all my friends, and myself in a line. The bouncers were bloodied up and very angry. Then the manager pointed at my dad and me saying, "Those are the two instigators." They arrested both of us and took us to the Multnomah County Jail. We rode together in the back of the police cruiser. I remember quoting a line from one of the Budweiser commercials to him, "I love you man." I would not see him again for three years.

He spent the next three-and-a-half years in prison. It was during this time in prison that he was truly set free (see Chapter 2), but that didn't help my situation. I was sitting in jail again, not knowing if I would be released for my wedding. What would my in-laws think? What was I thinking? How could I be so stupid? Fortunately, they cut me loose at 5 a.m.; I called Ken's girlfriend to pick me up and take me home. When I woke up on Friday morning, I explained to Gwenna what happened. She was both very angry and very relieved. Her anger was from the fact that I would do such a stupid thing right before our wedding and relieved that my dad wouldn't be attending. We spent the day finishing all the details of our wedding. This included contacting our friends to tell them the wedding was not cancelled.

On our wedding day, Gwenna looked amazing. She was truly a princess and I felt extremely blessed. I could not believe that I was finally getting married. I had my tuxedo, and my friend's wife applied my makeup. I needed makeup to cover up the bruising and wounds from the brawl. During our wedding, I almost passed out and my perspiration caused the makeup to run down my face. When it was all said and done, Gwenna and I were married at the Old Pioneer Church in Portland, Oregon. I was extremely proud to marry her, and we set off for a honeymoon in Maui. We had a wonderful time and returned home, ready to start a new life together.

Mr. & Mrs. Scott Bradley

We were living with my sisters and longed to buy a place of our own. The place where we were living belonged to my stepdad Gary, and he offered to sell it to us. He accepted our offer, and we purchased our first home. It felt like things were starting to go in our favor. During this time we purchased our second "son," a Schipperke named Martin.

We started attending the church where Gwenna was raised. I had a hard time connecting with people, and wasn't drawn to their worship style. I also struggled with being at church with her parents. I don't know why I felt this way; maybe I wanted my independence. After a few months, I quit going to church and started back into my old pattern of drinking every weekend. We purchased a couple quads, and I often went riding out of town.

Martin

I finally told Gwenna that I did not want anything to do with her church or her religion. I wanted to live life my way, and if she didn't like it, she could leave. We lived this way for several months. I also bought a new truck and maxed out our credit card buying accessories for it. She was not happy about that! However, we did find out that all the charges from my bachelor party incident had been dropped.

Our marriage changed during an argument over what we were doing with our lives. During this argument, I repeatedly yelled at her, demanding we get a divorce. She calmly said divorce was not an option. She wanted to work through all our problems. I told her divorce was an option, and began to feel trapped by our marriage. She continued telling me that we were not getting divorced and I needed to figure out what was wrong with me. Her words sent me over the edge and I pushed her onto the couch.

I stood over her, pointing my index finger in her face, and began to demean, criticize, and verbally assault her with a long list of profanity, "There isn't anything wrong with me. It's you! You're the one going around trying to change everybody. It's you! You're the one that's all messed up! It's you! It's you!" At that point, I looked into a mirror across the room and saw an image of a madman. I thought to myself, "I look just like my dad." I broke down and wept. I could not keep running from my past any longer. She held me, and we decided to seek help.

The first person I called was my mom. She offered counsel and support. Her marriage to Gary was one of stability and strength and I knew I could trust them. They took us out on their sailboat for the afternoon and let us just sit in peace. We talked about life and our struggles; from that day forward I committed to making real changes. I desperately wanted to change and become a man who loved his wife. I wanted to be free from the chains that had bound my soul for so long. Mom told us that we would find that freedom and forgiveness in Jesus. I asked Him to help us change.

"We must develop and maintain the capacity to forgive. He who is devoid of the power to forgive is devoid of the power to love. There is some good in the worst of us and some evil in the best of us."
Martin Luther King, Jr.

personal reflection

My wife is a rock. Her emotional stability kept us afloat while I was a sinking ship of emotional baggage. My mom always says that we balance each other out. I am the more emotional one and she possesses a balanced thought process. I am thankful for her commitment and desire to do life God's way. She showed me the love and grace of God when I could not see it anywhere else. She was, and still is, Jesus with skin on. She is my best friend and lover. I needed to take my eyes off me and put them on what really mattered.

"My (Jesus') command is this: Love each other as I have loved you. Greater love has no one than this: to lay down one's life for one's friends. You are my friends if you do what I command."
John 15:12-13

Ken & me at my wedding

ten

FROM ME TO WE

*"For this reason a man will leave his father and mother and be
united to his wife, and the two will become one flesh."*
Ephesians 5:31

The first thing I did was commit to stop drinking and partying all the
time. I also agreed to attend church with Gwenna. Gary advised me
to get involved with a men's accountability group. Those types of
groups helped him change and become the man he longed to be. So I
started attending church and got involved in a men's group. I began
asking God to change me and give me the courage to face my issues.
Gwenna and I began seeing a marriage counselor who helped us see
the impact of our choices and gave us tools to communicate better. I
started taking classes that addressed the addictive mindset and how to
set clear boundaries.

We were doing great and I had quit drinking for several months.
Then we flew down to Vegas for a friend's wedding. I decided to cut
loose and spent the entire time drunk and smoking pot. It felt like a
huge step backwards for me, and I kept socially drinking when we
returned home. I wasn't getting into barroom brawls anymore, but the
behaviors still had a grip on my life. So now I was attending church,
leading a men's group on sexual purity, and drinking socially.

Gwenna and I wanted to have a baby together, but she could not get
pregnant. We did all the testing, but no one could find anything wrong
with either of us. We decided to keep trying and trusting God. I
believe God wanted to do a work in my heart before allowing me be a
father.

I needed to stop and address the underlying issues in my life. I was
not really doing this at church or in my group. I continued to drink
with my friends, and God had to get my attention. He did it by

allowing me to get to the end of my chain. He got my attention at my friend's birthday party. We went out with a group of friends to have a few beers and celebrate his birthday. I ended up drunk and initiating a barroom brawl. The fight included many of the friends I was telling about Jesus and how much He had changed my life. It ended with me being restrained by a close friend whom I almost punched in the face. Gwenna and I left before the police arrived.

I remained clean, sober, and in recovery for close to 8 years. I thought drinking was my problem. It was not my problem; a broken belief system was the root issue. After releasing my drinking problem to God, I was able to begin addressing the root issues in my life. That's when things started to make sense. I learned that many of my problems were associated with past trauma. I began to understand that I had to deal with my false beliefs if I wanted to live a healthy life. The lies I believed were driving my self-destructive behavior. As I learned that I could trust God with all of me, Gwenna began trusting me again. During my counseling and small group work, I had to address the abuse and trauma of my past. I could not keep running from the pain. I had to tell the truth about how much it hurt to grow up in a broken home. I had to tell the truth about the scars and wounds from my past. I had to open up the extremely painful events of my past so they could heal. I addressed my poor choices and the hurt done to me. I had to talk about the sexual abuse and how it affected my life.

changed beliefs = changed behaviors

Gwenna did not understand most of what I was going through. She had never experienced the abuse, trauma, or feelings that I experienced. So when I took a class on healing from childhood sexual abuse, she had to let me process. I was extremely vulnerable at this time. I remember her gently rubbing my back one night at our home, and I jumped out of the bed. In my mind, I had instantly returned to the dark room with my uncle trying to seduce me. The trauma was deep and painful.

With tenderness and patience, she helped me process my feelings. She began to understand the truth about PTSD (Post Traumatic Stress Disorder). I had to talk through the lies I believed about others and myself. I had to intentionally forgive and allow God to become the judge. I developed strong boundaries and courage through the journey.

This opened up a door to minister to countless other victims and survivors of abuse.

We continued serving in ministry; then God opened up the door for us to help plant a church in Sunnyside, Oregon. It was an amazing adventure that brought many people to Jesus. We led Bible studies and helped every Sunday. Shane Sullivan, the preaching pastor, became one of my best friends. On top of that, Gwenna finally became pregnant with our first daughter, Maicee.

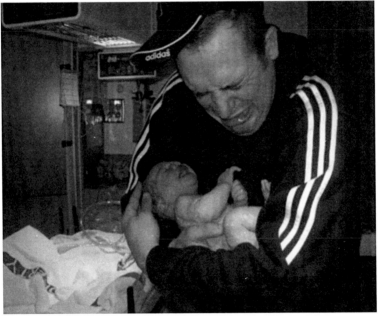

The joy of becoming a father! Maicee's birth in March 2003

I was so proud to be a father and a man of God. I longed to be the man who led with courage and strength. I wanted to live like Jesus and grow in my understanding of our heavenly Father. I started to believe the truth of how God saw me: His adopted son, apple of His eye, and pleased with me. I felt stronger than ever, and knew that God was at the center of our lives. I didn't say we had arrived. We still had our normal arguments, but it was nothing like we had experienced before. I allowed mentors and other men to speak into my life. They taught me how to be a man, and modeled what a family should be. Three in particular impacted me: Mickey Malkus, Shane Sullivan, and Greg Woods. I am so thankful to God for allowing me to experience the love of honorable men during that season of my life.

After irreconcilable differences in our church plant, Shane resigned and moved his family to California. Shortly after that, I believed God was calling us in a different direction. The thing He most impressed upon my heart was the call to be a pastor. I could not stop thinking or talking about Jesus. It didn't matter where we went or what we did, I wanted people to hear and understand how much God loves them. He had forgiven me, so He could forgive anyone. That is Good News for everyone! My life changed when I received the grace and mercy of God. Nothing else had come close!

During this time of transition, I started writing my dad in prison. He told me that he was a changed man, but I was leery. I had heard it too many times before. So I drove to the prison to see him face-to-face.

When the guards brought him through the courtyard and into the mess hall, I looked into his eyes. This was not the same man I knew. He had a light in his eyes that illuminated the entire room.

As I went up to greet him, he

Visiting Dad in prison in 2003

took me in his arms and said, "I love you son. I love you and I'm so sorry." I was paralyzed by love and wept in his arms. I could not believe that this was my dad. He was a changed man! I was praising God. So instead of talking about all the "war stories" of our past, we praised God for two days as brothers in Christ. We were no longer separated by the sins of our past but were now men of God.

doing the right thing

When Dad returned home, he reunited with his family. He found out that my uncle was still involved in child abuse. We both loved my uncle and wanted to see him find help. The pain that he was causing other children and families was unacceptable. He had charges pending for molestation. The prosecution needed another victim to give a statement. I decided to share my story. That led to him being treated at the Oregon State Mental Hospital. I did not do this out of revenge or malice, but out of love. I had already forgiven my uncle and wanted to help him. I also did not want any more children being exposed to his malicious behavior. He had a problem and needed professional assistance.

You may wonder how I could forgive him. I realized that I needed to forgive him to set myself free. An important aspect of forgiveness involves placing clear boundaries between our perpetrators and ourselves. I applied these boundaries through the support and encouragement from other family members, groups, and counselors. I have learned that I must have others in my life to move forward as a healthy individual. As I established these clear boundaries, I realized I was not vulnerable to be hurt by him again. This enables me to love him as God does. I allow God to be judge and prosecutor. He knows what will help my uncle change from the inside out. I continue to pray for him and trust God to change his life.

During this time, my family started attending another church and felt right at home. We started helping by leading classes on marriage. I really loved the vision of the church and pastoral staff. We invested several years as volunteer leaders, building relationships and caring for people. I was the overseer of all recovery and restoration ministries. My heart was drawn to the broken and hurting people struggling with addictions and pain. I realized that God gives us our greatest ministry out of our greatest agony. I loved seeing people transformed by the living God. Jesus Christ was changing lives, and I felt fulfilled.

Not long after this, Gwenna became pregnant with our second daughter, Sophie. I was so happy to expand the love of our family.

Life couldn't get any better. God had given me what I had dreamt of: a beautiful and caring wife, two amazing daughters, a home, and a great career. I felt a sense of contentment, except for the call to be a pastor. I knew in my heart that God wanted me to become a pastor; I tried to wait patiently for His leading. I believed He would be faithful to complete what He began in my heart.

Finally it happened! I was invited to join the staff of our church as pastor of the new campus being launched in Northeast Portland. Gwenna and I felt blessed and released to move forward. We led a healthy, balanced life. I had a productive ten-year career that included a lucrative salary and benefit package. I knew leaving this job and

Sophie Ann Bradley

financial security and trusting God in ministry was a leap of faith. This transition was made easier because my employer was offering buyouts for early retirees. I was able to take advantage of this and pay off a few bills before beginning our new season of life. God was amazing in His leading to the next season of our lives. We were excited!

What I didn't realize was the faithfulness of our Heavenly Father. He was about to teach me deeper life lessons on being a man of integrity, husband, father, leader, and true disciple of Jesus Christ.

dream come true

I joined the staff of our church on October 1, 2008. I was officially a pastor and ready to share the Good News with anyone who would listen! I was excited to help launch the new campus and build a team to support this vision. I prayed to God that all of our closest friends and ministry leaders would feel called to help reach people for Christ. In addition, God was faithful in preparing the hearts of our friends and family to join us. As we came together to do His work, He brought out the best in so many people. We had a big task and needed His blessing all the way.

Since our church facility was a donated building that needed remodeling, one of my first responsibilities was to lead the remodeling project. I accepted this task and longed to do a great job, but I was scared to death. I had never led a project like this before. I also had to learn many of the pastoral care duties through on-the-job training. I had never facilitated a memorial service or wedding, but knew I was called to it.

God was faithful to surround me with encouraging staff, volunteers, and leadership. Several families and members of the church that previously owned the building joined in helping with this project. These people had amazing insights into the culture and demographic of that particular community. I was especially eager to collaborate with friends and family from our restoration ministry team. Many of these people had come out of some incredibly difficult life circumstances to find faith and fulfillment in Christ. They were ready to join hands and serve Northeast Portland together. Many had been clean and sober for only a short period of time.

In 2009, I was also blessed to go on my first motorcycle ride with my dad and brother Chance. On our way to Lake Tahoe, we rode through California and spoke at a youth retreat. We shared about the power of God to change lives, and several kids gave their lives to Christ.

personal reflection

I was truly having a mountaintop experience. God had brought to reality my dream of becoming a pastor. I felt love and support from everyone in my life. I was blessed with a beautiful family and amazing friends. I didn't know how life could have gotten any better. If you don't believe in miracles, now is the time to start re-thinking your position on God's divine intervention.

Me with Dad and Chance

eleven

LIVING THE DREAM

"I have told you these things, so that in me you may have peace. In this world you will have trouble. But take heart! I have overcome the world."
The words of Jesus in John 16:33

After being on the pastoral staff for a few weeks, I joined the other eight pastors for a retreat at the beach. I was excited to get away and start building relationships with these guys. I hoped to gain insight and wisdom during our prayer and study time and anticipated a wonderful experience hanging out with them. The other pastors had unique personalities and lively spirits. I was committed to soaking up everything that God was offering me.

Upon arrival, we stopped by the supermarket to purchase food and supplies including a couple cases of beer and several bottles of wine. When we returned to our rental home, we settled in for the night. It had a nice hot tub, pool table, and big screen TV. It was a man's paradise. When everyone finished putting their stuff in their rooms, we came together for prayer. We prayed for the church, our families, and our ministries. After that, a few of the guys hit the hot tub while others played pool and watched TV. Several of them decided to have a glass of wine or a beer.

They offered me a beer and I had a choice: be true to myself or fit in. Based on my fear of not being accepted, I decided to have a beer. I desperately wanted to be liked by my peers. I also felt I had resolved all my root issues that made me act like a drunken sailor. It was obvious to me that the "in" crowd of our group enjoyed consuming alcoholic beverages. It was my first beer in almost eight years. The intense feeling of shame consumed my heart, so I followed that beer with a few more. The pain was not from drinking, but from my lack of integrity as a leader. I just broke eight years of integrity and trust with the people I ministered to in recovery. I was able to escape those shameful feelings by drinking with the other pastors for the remainder of the retreat. We drank three out of the four days we were at the beach. We had a great time playing golf and cards, and also visited a local casino.

As we were getting ready to come home, we debriefed the weekend's events. I broke down in tears and explained the pain in my heart in having broken my sobriety. I told them how I hurt and wouldn't know what to tell my wife or the people I ministered to. They basically sat in silence not knowing how to support me.

The ride back to Portland was a somber one. When I returned home I told my wife what we had done; she did not seem too disturbed by my actions. It wasn't as if I got totally wasted and into a fight or something. When I returned to my men's group and explained what happened, they could not believe their ears. "How could you drink again," asked several of my accountability brothers. I decided to minimize my actions, and told them it was nothing. I explained that I had addressed all the issues in my life that previously caused me to abuse substances. I knew I had let them down, but decided that socially drinking was worth the inner turmoil I was experiencing.

We launched the church services on Easter 2008. As I look back on our first Easter Service, tears come to my eyes. The building was packed with people. I loved seeing all the children coming to learn about Jesus. Many people said "yes" to Jesus. We opened the baptismal and several people were baptized.

The first person baptized was my dear friend, Thad Williams. When he came out of the water raising his arms in praise to God, I was leveled emotionally. God was doing an amazing work and it was only the first public service. We launched the campus with positive momentum. It brought me great pleasure to see my family and close friends rise up into positions of leadership. We were on a mission to reach our city for Jesus Christ. Each one of us was learning a lot about sacrificially serving others and leading an organization. They were exciting times with many wonderful memories. As the church progressed, my drinking slowly turned into a pattern. Instead of spending my downtime practicing spiritual disciplines, I was looking for the next event when I could hang out with my buddies. My wife seemed to enjoy the newfound freedom I had, and we experienced many good times together drinking in moderation. We went out a lot and spent time on vacations to the beach, Mexico, and Las Vegas.

The church was growing, and I was gaining confidence as a leader. I had many wonderful experiences speaking in front of thousands of people, sharing the good news of Jesus Christ. I was mentoring many families and friends. God was bringing people from every walk of life. I absolutely loved it, but the undercurrent of shame never left my side. Pride began to enslave me and I started to harden inside. I turned all recovery and restoration ministries over to another pastor. It hurt to hear people talking and rejecting me as a hypocrite.

My biggest issue wasn't the drinking; it was leadership development. Drinking was not my primary problem; it was getting my eyes off of Jesus. I was learning how to manage a large organization, not implementing spiritual disciplines. This killed me more than the pain of rejection from others. I felt like I was rejecting God. He calls us to make disciples, not man-made kingdoms.

Even though I was leading and involved with many people, I slowly started to die inside. I began spending time with people who valued different things. Learning business management techniques and leadership principles became more important than leading others to follow Jesus. The sad part is I really wanted to be true to myself, but felt I could not be. I was living a double life and I thought nobody knew it except me. I'm sure it was obvious to everyone else.

During this time a strong group of friends blessed me. I had their support and encouragement as I made "another trip around the barn." One friend in particular, Charles DeKar, became my closest confidant and he has become my best friend (outside of Gwenna). He continues to be a man I admire and trust.

I felt like I was living within a double bind. I was damned if I did change and damned if I did not change. I was afraid to expose my feelings to the men that I admired, so I continued to go with the flow. The most influential person in my life was our senior pastor. I grew to love him and viewed him as a father figure, but it seemed the only quality time I spent with him was out on the town. We enjoyed riding our motorcycles and going out with our friends, and we usually had a great time together. I don't believe he realized the influence he had on my life. My greatest desire was to model his leadership and become successful as a pastor. Our friendship led to planning a motorcycle run to Sturgis. We were excited to experience a great trip with several of our closest friends. This vacation never took place.

Despite my emotional struggles, I learned so much. I was the officiating pastor for many weddings and memorial services. I also helped organize large events that met the needs of our community. I was asked to speak at various events and mentor young leaders. I became friends and peers with many of Portland's faith-based leaders. We developed plans to bring change and reform into Northeast Portland. I was on several boards and helped launch citywide campaigns for change. United in our efforts, we helped bring change to our community. God was growing me as a man and leader despite my internal battles. I hope you'll agree that God continues to work through us, even when we make mistakes. As a matter of fact, He does His best work with broken people. God uses the weak to show His strengths. The beauty of His presence is in transformation. The best evangelism is a changed life. He amazes me all the time!

Another blessing was seeing my sister Sada graduate from college. She is the first person in our family to complete this goal and move on to graduate courses. Way to go, Sada!

You may wonder if I neglected my family during this busy time of my life. I can honestly say that I did not. I made a commitment at the beginning of our call to full-time ministry to put family first. I never missed an important event or school function. I was home most evenings with my family. I was physically present and emotionally connected, while taking pride in my relationship with them. They encouraged me as a husband and father. God continues to reveal His love and care for me through my family. Being a father has helped me understand God's role in my life.

I stayed true to my lifelong commitment in honoring my wife. Sexual purity is high on my priority list, especially since I've experienced sexual addiction and seen the pain that promiscuity presents. It destroys lives and hurts the family.

don't ask, don't tell

This next season was extremely difficult for me. I was invited to join two other pastors for a creative team retreat to plan and prepare the series of messages for the coming year. We spent several days working hard to finish our list of goals. On the final evening of the retreat, we went out to dinner and then back to our room. We had a couple drinks and then ventured to the hot tub located in the recreation area. Twenty minutes later we were joined by another group of people in the hot tub. This group included a married couple and two single women. After thirty minutes of small talk our entire group decided to meet at a local bar for drinks.

We were having a nice time visiting with our new friends. I explained to them that we were pastors from a church in Portland. They were intrigued by the fact that we would hang out in a bar with them. We tried to explain that God doesn't call us to be religious extremists, but asks us to be in relationship with Him and He accepts us just as we are. This conversation sat well with them. As the DJ appeared on stage, he encouraged the crowd to come up and sing karaoke. We took turns singing our favorite songs and everyone was having a great time. That's when I noticed one of the women from our group getting very friendly with our senior pastor. This escalated to them slow dancing during several songs. The singing and dancing continued for a couple hours, until the owner of the bar announced that it was closing time. As our group was leaving, the associate pastor explained that we had drunk enough and should leave. The senior pastor and I told him he could leave, and we would catch up with him later. He was visibly frustrated and left us there while he returned to our hotel room.

Our group ventured to the tavern next door. We sat in the bar swapping stories and meeting new people. I noticed the same woman and the senior pastor getting uncomfortably close to each other. I went to his table and tried to reason with him, but he didn't listen. I was filled with fear and realized that a huge moral line had been crossed. We were called to be leaders for God, not a couple of drunks sitting in a bar entertaining women. When I returned to the table after paying our bill, others at the table told me he left with the woman. I anxiously walked down the street looking for my friend at every intersection. I didn't know where they were or what they were doing. What was he thinking? Where did they go? What was happening? We were supposed to be responsible shepherds of a growing mega-church. Instead, we were acting like reckless teenage boys without a care in the world. I called and texted him several times, but he never responded. I realized there wasn't anything I could do and went to bed.

I didn't know what to say as our pastor group ate breakfast the next morning and prepared to return home. Not much was said until halfway home, when the senior pastor told us he could not remember what happened after he left the tavern. He also explained that he was deeply remorseful for his actions. We tried to console him, but I struggled with what to say. After a long discussion, we agreed not to talk to anyone about the activities from the previous night. The reasoning behind that decision was to not burden our families or the church body with our poor choices. I knew keeping this secret was wrong, but believed we would lose our jobs if anyone found out what had taken place.

When we returned home, it was business as usual. No one mentioned the events of the retreat. My anxiety grew. I lived in fear that someone would find out. The other pastors acted as if nothing ever happened. The choice to keep this a secret finalized my decision to resign from my position as a pastor. I just couldn't take any more secrets or dysfunctional behavior. I had bought into the lie of "image-management." I became more interested in how people viewed me, and less interested in who I was becoming as a man. The stress of keeping my game-face on was overwhelming. I needed to change. It got to the point where I couldn't look in the mirror without hating what I saw. I was making poor choices. The shame of our secrecy was destroying me. I despised myself and couldn't look other people in the eyes, especially the senior pastor's wife. I was as sick as my secrets.

In my heart I knew it was time to leave full-time ministry. I did not want to resign, but I was slowly dying inside. I understood that I had been given a great opportunity to serve God and others, but I desperately needed to change. I had to accept the fact that the decisions I was making were suffocating me spiritually and draining me emotionally. It was a daily battle within my heart. Despite my inconsistencies, God continued doing amazing things in our church. He's so much bigger than our problems.

resignation

I finally resigned in May of 2010. I needed time to rest and figure out what happened to me. I applied for a position with my former employer, the telephone company. When I informed the senior pastor of my intention to resign, he seemed relieved. This really bothered me. When I explained my desire to resign to our executive pastor (who had not been on the retreat), he wanted more details. Since I wasn't ready to talk about my true reason, I told him I needed a break from the rigors of full-time ministry. He proceeded to inform the elders.

After that, I received a report that one of the elders accused me of valuing money over ministry. This did not sit well with me and I decided to tell the truth. I explained what had happened at the retreat and the enormous toll it took on my life. I told them about everything I had experienced and dealt with. In disclosing this, I felt like I betrayed the other pastors, but knew in my heart that the truth would set us free. After many meetings and conversations, no one agreed on what took place. The eldership implemented change in staff and procedures. It was a very difficult time for our church. The elders accepted my resignation and blessed me on my journey. I followed up with counseling and accountability with our executive pastor. He was a rock through this whole process, and has been a mentor and dear friend. The decision to resign and do the right thing was the most difficult thing I have ever done. I felt like I was letting my lifelong dream slip away. The right thing to do is always the hard thing to do. Resigning was the right thing to do.

I believe this decision also saved my marriage. Living a life of secrecy and isolation was taking me down a dark road. I knew in my heart that if I did not leave I would eventually lose it all. I also knew it would probably escalate if I went on that motorcycle trip with my friends. I may have slept with another woman or used drugs or something worse. The stress and anxiety had consumed my life. At that point in my life, anything was possible!

I took being a pastor very seriously. I knew God had called me to lead well and influence people for His glory. I fell short and publicly asked for forgiveness. I did not want to miss the opportunity to share my heart. My deepest desire was to make amends with the precious people whom I loved dearly. I also approached other friends and family privately. This allowed me to connect at a deeper level and share my heart. Even though I did all the right things, I still felt guilty for not doing a better job.

After my resignation, I entered into a deep depression. I believed I lost my lifelong dream. It hurt beyond description. I soon detached from everyone, even my wife. After I was re-hired by the phone company, my employer sent me out of town for training a couple weeks per month. I was miserable sitting in my hotel room alone. I thought about all my problems while watching television. I was consumed with thinking about my broken dreams and messed up life. That is when I chose to visit a casino and began gambling. It was a great way to escape my pain (hopefully you read the sarcasm). It temporarily removed my sense of worthlessness. Nevertheless, the wagers grew, and I did not tell Gwenna about my impulsive behavior.

This lasted about three months, until I had spent everything we had and racked up a large debt on our credit card. We could barely pay our bills, and I had to tell her what was happening. She was extremely disappointed in me. She could not believe that I would jeopardize the financial stability of our family through such frivolous behavior. She did not know that gambling became a problem for me. I felt like I was back to being the "old me."

She didn't realize that I was dying inside. I believed I had lost everything, including my dreams and reasons for living. I put so much of my life into being a pastor, only to throw it away with erratic behavior. My self-hatred grew to an alarming level. I honestly thought about running away, divorcing my wife, and never coming back. When I tried to explain this to the pastors at our church they were more interested in moving on and did not seem to listen to my heartfelt cries for help. This hurt me deeply, and, once again, reminded me that I was on my own.

I felt like I had let everyone down. My kids were the only bright light in my life. We tried not to fight in front of them, but they noticed. They asked us why we were fighting all the time. They had never witnessed this before. I hurt Gwenna deeply, and we both sought counseling. How could she forgive me again?

personal reflection

This was the hardest chapter to write. Admitting that I lost my dream job and then hurting my wife again is not easy. It is much simpler to write from an "arrived" perspective. God gave me so much to build on, and I felt like I destroyed the foundation. After leaving ministry, I fell into one of my darkest bouts with depression and self-rejection. I had a difficult time seeing that God could still have a plan for my life. I thought His plan had been completed, and I didn't live up to my end of the bargain. I know I hardened my heart and became stiff-necked to my critics. Maybe that transferred over to my relationship with Him.

In the confession of concrete sins the old man dies a painful, shameful death before the eyes of a brother. Because this humiliation is so hard, we continually scheme to avoid it. Yet in the deep mental and physical pain of humiliation before our brother we experience the cross of Jesus as our rescue and salvation. The old man dies, but it is God who has conquered him. Now we share in the resurrection of Christ and eternal life.
Dietrich Bonheoffer

twelve

DEATH TO LIFE

"Listen carefully: Unless a grain of wheat is buried in the ground, dead to the world, it is never any more than a grain of wheat. But if it is buried, it sprouts and reproduces itself many times over. In the same way, anyone who holds on to life just as it is destroys that life. But if you let it go, reckless in your love, you'll have it forever, real and eternal."
John 12:23-25 (MSG)

Once again, I realized I must die to self so that I might live again. I needed God's healing touch in my life. This time it would not be in the public eye or serving others in ministry. God wanted to do a work in me. In His faithfulness, He provided wise counsel for me in the form of a non-profit gambling counselor. Gwenna and I had a few friends who had seen him for their issues.

Before our first meeting, I had already decided that he could not really help me. I thought, "What's this guy going to teach me that I haven't already done or taught others a hundred times?" I went to see him full of pride while drowning in self-pity. It was during our first session that I began to understand God's amazing grace. He shared with me that he, too, shared a similar past and found healing through Jesus Christ. I am not sure if he was supposed to tell me this since he was a state sanctioned counselor. But we hit it off, and I learned to trust him with my life.

After I told him my story and why I wanted help, he asked me what I thought my problem was. I told him the basics. I explained that I use problematic behaviors to anesthetize the pain in my life. He agreed but wanted to dig deeper. He asked me to look at the issue of pride in my life. He wanted to know what role that played in my misery. I told him that I would address it and ask God to remove it from my life. I learned that God does not "remove" pride from people. They must release it.

I became acutely aware that I had become an extremely prideful person. Humility was not on my radar. Pride was protecting me from being hurt by others, but it also kept me from receiving the help I desperately needed. It also kept me safe from being exposed as a fraud or hypocrite. I enjoyed being seen as someone who had it together. As I began addressing this issue in my life, things started to change. I spent more time praying and reading God's Word. I began treating others with empathy and compassion. I started to see and feel the pain that I had caused my wife and others. I hurt again, but this time it was the pain of repentance.

In my pride and self-pity, I was self-centered. In removing that plank from my eye, I began to see the pain my wife was carrying. Not necessarily the pain of my choices, but the hurt of leaving our church and of making other life transitions. I began to feel for her again. I also had to address my critical attitude towards the church leadership. I spent many hours judging the decisions and motives of those in leadership. Some of my concerns were valid, but I was not positioned to be the change agent. While I was trying to remove the speck of sawdust from everyone else's eye, it became clear that I had a huge plank protruding out of my face. As my relationship grew with God and my counselor, I started to see hope. The hope came from the change in my attitude and relationship with Him. After I made a decision to grieve the loss of my dreams, God revealed that He is not done with me yet.

My wife and I began attending our church again. Most of our friends remained at the church and continued serving God. I released myself not to lead or be in a position of control. This allowed us to be led by God, not committed to leading others. We felt comfortable in this position until it became apparent that it was not a healthy place for us. I had a difficult time with the decisions being made behind the scenes. It was extremely alarming to watch the senior leaders and elders make decisions without informing the church body of what was really going on. They were divided on how to proceed. I believe they wanted to see healthy changes take place in leadership, but image-management and control were more important. Everything was presented in a positive light to the congregation. We decided to remove our family from membership and begin a new journey. The most difficult challenge in leaving was realizing that we would not see our friends and church family as often.

personal reflection

This season opened up a brand new relationship with my parents and friends. It led to me writing this book and returning to college to finish my bachelor's degree. God is good. He is faithful to forgive and love us! I am also blessed to know that Chance, Sada, and Star all follow Christ. I realize now that I am still living the dream and am hopeful for a bright future with God by my side. As I have written my story I've been overwhelmed by God's faithfulness. He has given me a beautiful bride who loves me unconditionally. He has placed two wonderful daughters in my care. It brings me to tears to think of the love they have for each other. My position within the phone company allows for a lot of time to reflect, pray, and contemplate my life. Life is good. I am looking forward to our trip to Disneyland. God is good.

You may be asking, "So what does this have to do with forgiveness?" I would say, "Everything." If we cannot forgive ourselves, others, and God, we will be filled with resentment, pride, and contempt. If we can't receive forgiveness from others and God, we will live lonely, isolated lives searching for meaning and affirmation from the world.

Forgiveness begins with allowing ourselves to be courageous, vulnerable, and trusting. Forgiveness gives us the ability to trust again. Learning to trust again is the beginning of life. Through a relationship with Jesus Christ, we can learn to trust from the depths of our souls. He is the Forgiveness Factor. He doesn't stop loving us when we make mistakes. He walks beside us and empowers us to change.

As I wrap up this chapter I'd like to share how I am resolving to be a different man. I now seek accountability relationships through counseling and a men's group. I am honest and open with my wife in all areas of my life. I am especially sensitive to anything that appears secretive or deceiving. This has helped eliminate the stress and anxiety of trying to remember each detail of half-truths and blatant lies.

I spent six months in solitude and prayer before writing this book. This meant laying aside all ministry commitments and leadership roles. I re-connected with God. In my time alone with him I was able to hear His voice again. I read the Bible daily and also spend time reading books by Christian authors and leaders. God uses His Word and the words of other authors to mentor and shape me into a disciple of Jesus Christ. I also set clear boundaries with my time and energy. My wife appreciates the newfound connection we have. Although the pain of the past still arises, we are healing through the daily commitment to change. My children are blessed to know that their father is fighting for character and integrity.

Two other choices have helped me move forward. One is to stop procrastinating. I chose to write this book and return to college to complete my bachelor's degree. The other is volunteering at a local rescue mission. As I serve the men of the program one night a week, I am learning to appreciate the value of life and the unique contributions of each individual. The men are precious and inspire me to want to be a passionate follower of Jesus Christ. Their authenticity and transparency are definitely a breath of fresh air.

"But God demonstrates his own love for us in this: While we were still sinners Christ died for us."
                              Romans 5:8

thirteen

THE FORGIVENESS FACTOR

"This is love: not that we loved God, but that he loved us and sent his Son as an atoning sacrifice for our sins. Dear friends, since God so loved us, we also ought to love one another. No one has ever seen God; but if we love one another, God lives in us and his love is made complete in us."
1 John 4:10-12

Writing this book has brought tremendous healing into my life. The greatest fruit came in realizing how blessed I am today. I have spent years resenting myself for my poor choices. And just when I thought all hope was gone, God showed up to redeem my broken spirit. I am living the dream, His dream. I thought I missed my chance, but His plan has been in place for eternity. I just didn't have eyes to see it. Experiencing hard times is not for the purpose of breaking us, but to strengthen us. It hasn't been easy, but it has been well worth it.

Processing my historical trauma revealed a massive wound in my soul that researchers and psychologists identify as a father wound. It began with my father, stepfathers, and authority figures. They did not protect, invest, and nurture my soul. They wounded me and in return, I learned to survive in unhealthy ways. I learned not to trust anyone, including God. This developed into a belief system that I used to protect myself. When I did open the door to male relationships, it was met with further rejection, abuse, and pain. I desperately wanted to believe in people, but usually was left wondering where the real fathers were. This pattern of relationships has continued throughout my life.

Besides the pain of not feeling loved, I wounded others. In our church and various ministries I hurt the hurting because of my lack of integrity and connectedness. I carry this reality with a heavy heart. During a counseling session with Dr. Ted Roberts, founder of Pure Desire Ministries International, I tried to explain the depth of pain that I felt for being a hypocrite. He said, "Son, you are not a hypocrite.

You are wounded. You can be healed and liberated as you trust God to be your Father. Men will let you down, but God never fails. As you move forward, bond with healthy men that lead with integrity, honesty, and compassion." Those words helped set me free.

My family is reconciled. Mom, Dad, and I all live in harmony because of Jesus. I feel blessed by learning more about my parents and their journeys. The love and compassion I feel for them has changed the ways I respond to them. We've shared our stories and ministered to our communities. My prayer is that my siblings will see our parents through God's eyes.

Looking at my own life and patterns of behavior has helped me re-focus on God. I am committed to spiritual growth and applying biblical principles to my life. This new season of life has allowed me to get out of the public eye and spend time with Him. I have been refreshed with a newness of life.

forgiving myself

Today I forgive me. I have done horrible things and hurt many people. Time and again, I have made a mess of my life. Today I stand on God's vision for my life. He loves me, and I can learn to love myself. I am the apple of His eye. No more false vows and lies. I stand on God's truth as witnessed in Jesus Christ.

We all make mistakes, but it's how we handle those mistakes that make us people of integrity. When I choose to hide, lie, or manage my life outside of God's truth, I once again begin a trip down a path of destruction. I want to be a follower of Christ who is authentic, transparent, and able to stand on the truth of His unfailing love. As God transforms me to becoming more like Christ, I find myself living beyond my past mistakes and taking refuge in His refining love and mercy. I can stand upright and not be ashamed of who I am or where I've been.

I have value and worth. I am not alone. I am loved. I am a man of God. I am blessed with a loving, forgiving wife and two amazing daughters who have all shown me the love of God. I am thankful for my past, from birth to today, which has made me the loving, compassionate, empathetic, and strong man that I am. I will take up the Sword of the Spirit (God's Word) and continue the fight. I'm a child of God!

a message for my wife

Gwenna has loved me with an everlasting love. She sees the best in me and never doubted my potential. She didn't stop there. She expects me to fulfill God's plan for my life. She expects me to be a great father and husband. She expects me to grow to full maturation. She expects me to honor my commitments. She has helped me become the man I am today. Countless times I have hurt her and betrayed her trust; I am thankful she sees my heart and knows my intentions are to live for God. She is an angel and deserves my praise. I love her. She is an amazing and talented mother. I believe our daughters are blessed because of her love.

I am learning to love my wife as Christ loves the church. I desire to lay down my life for her. I pray I can show daughters the love I have received from Christ. Since He is our perfect Father, I find great satisfaction in knowing God is teaching me how to be a father.

friends & family

I am thankful for all of my friends and family. Without them life would be extremely difficult. They have helped bring light to the dark places of my life. I hope I can do the same for you.

PS: The trip to Disneyland was awesome!

fourteen
THE BLESSING

God is good. There is no doubt about it. No matter where you've been or what you've done, God can change your life. If you've been chewed up and spit out on life's highway, let me remind you that you have a heavenly Father who deeply loves you. He has plans you can't comprehend. He works in ways that you and I will never understand. He is a good Father.

hearing the words

After returning from Disneyland, I received a message from a childhood friend. She asked me if I had ever contacted the victim of the assault I was involved with twenty years ago. I wrote of this earlier in the book; the young man was permanently injured and I fled the scene because I thought I had killed him. I wrote about spending time in jail, which included my eighteenth birthday, and a felony assault conviction. I carried a heavy load of guilt and shame for twenty years because of the pain I caused this young man and his family. Each time I returned to my hometown, friends and their families would remind me of the hate and disgust that the victim's family had towards me.

I told my friend that I hadn't heard from or seen him since the day I was arrested, and that I'd always longed to make amends and ask for forgiveness. She told me she was friends with him and asked if I wanted her to give him my information through a social networking site. I was extremely excited and knew God was behind this amazing opportunity. I told her I needed to think about it, but immediately fired up my laptop and found him on the website. I sent him this message:

> Hi, XXXXXX,
>
> This is Scott Bradley, and I was one of the idiots that brawled with you back in 1991. My life has had its ups and downs but I have always felt

ashamed and disgusted by the way I acted in Klamath Falls, especially towards our altercation. It was wrong and I am deeply sorry. I would love to meet with you and share face-to-face from my heart. A lot has changed in twenty years. My email address is scott.bradley73@gmail.com and phone # is XXX-XXX-XXXX. I live near Portland and hope to hear back from you soon. It would mean a lot to me.

Thank you,
Scott

I prayerfully hoped he would accept my apology. The next day he contacted me:

Hey Scott,

You know, I wasn't sure how I was going to respond to your message after initially reading it, but you know what? I forgave you a long time ago. I was pissed and angry for quite a while and must have played the scenario over and over in my mind 100 times wondering where I went wrong....The doctors didn't even know for 11 days if I was going to be able to keep my right eye....

I became a Christian many years ago and learned that I had to let all of that anger go. It was doing me no good bottled up inside me, and it was actually harming me. Like I said earlier, I forgave you. We all make mistakes and Lord knows I've made many in my life. All we can do is try to learn from them and not make the same mistakes again...

In a way, I have you to thank for the life I have now. If that incident hadn't happened, I probably would have kept partying and would have wound up in jail. Instead, you gave me the urge to get in the military and out of Klamath. I've now been in since 1991, and just hit my 20-year mark this month. I've been a recruiter for the last 11 years, so you are indirectly responsible for me being able to help and enlist over 200 people since I started....

When I first met my wife, we dated for six months before marriage. She is the most awesome and wonderful person in my life, and again... if that hadn't happened, I may not have ever met her. I also wouldn't have had the son, now 14, that I have today. I believe I actually owe you thanks. You helped straighten my life out....I see you have a beautiful family yourself. Congrats! I hope all is well with you, and thanks for sending the message.

Well, take care, and don't worry about the past, only learn from it.

XXXXXX

I beat myself up over my actions for twenty years. Even after I trusted God with my life and received His forgiveness through Christ, I continued seeing a broken man in the mirror because of my past mistakes. I longed to make amends with this man (and many others) and then it finally happened. When he said, "I forgave you long ago," I realized that I've had an extremely difficult time forgiving myself.

We actually spoke on the phone and re-visited our journeys. I wept as he re-told of the pain and forgiveness he expressed to me. At the end of our phone conversation, he said, "Forgive yourself." This wasn't the first time I heard this. I made amends with several others and each time they told me, "I forgave you a long time ago, forgive yourself." (The best part was that he didn't know I was a Christian or a pastor; it was totally a God thing!)

God showed me that I am forgiven. God is good and able to break through our hardened hearts. I've always felt peace and joy in forgiving those who've hurt or sinned against me, but I'm experiencing an entirely different depth of love and peace now. When someone you've hurt deeply says, and means, "You are forgiven," it destroys the lies that keep you bound. Three words destroyed the lie I believed about myself. That lie was: "You are your past." The Truth that set me free is this: "You are forgiven."

fighting for the hearts of men

I decided it was time to spend more time with my dad. God had done a great healing in our lives but we needed more time together. I told him I would commit to visiting him once per quarter in our hometown. I would drive down, hang out, and go with him to the jail to minister to the inmates. I thought it would be cool as a father/son duo to fight for the hearts of these men. The experience would change my life.

On my way to our first weekend together, I had a lot of time to reflect on all that God had done. It is a five-hour drive from Portland to Klamath Falls. I was a bit anxious because this would be the first weekend where I actually just went to hang out with him. No real agenda—the only thing planned was the jail visit.

When we had dinner with some of his friends, I noticed that Dad was obviously the leader with this group. His leadership was based on his character and integrity. I saw people looking up to him and trusting him. He prayed over every meal and treated his wife with tenderness and humility. He spoke gently to others and always brought honor to God in his words. I was deeply moved by his transformation.

After dinner we reported to the jail. I was so excited I could hardly stand it. We met a couple of the volunteers and prayed for our time with the inmates. We asked God to use us to touch the hearts of the men and prayed that some would come to know Jesus as Lord and Savior. We asked God to move the mountains of pain, resentment, and confusion that had trapped these men for so long. We believed that God was willing and able to do just that!

We were scheduled for two ministry sessions, one in each of the men's housing pods. Our first session started off with a bang. As we were waiting to enter into our volunteer cell, one of the extremely large Native Americans got in my face and referenced my tattoos saying, "Tattoos. An F'n abomination to God!" One of the guards quickly asked him to move on. My dad looked at me to see if I was OK. I nodded that everything was cool, but inside I was trembling with fear and excitement. This was awesome! I was ready to fight for the hearts of these men.

When we entered the first cell meeting area, eight to ten men joined us. They sat on the floor on mats around us. It was obvious that several of the men knew my dad. They had either met him in the jail or on one of his work crews. Each of them had given their lives to Jesus through his ministry. Then there were several others who were checking out the "Bible study." I was quiet through the first part of the meeting, letting Dad facilitate the discussion.

He said a few words and then asked if everyone in the room was born again. That wasn't my style by any means and I was wondering why he was so "in their face" with his presentation of the Gospel. Most of the guys said "yes," but a couple of them weren't sure if they had been born again. As they talked back and forth, it was apparent a couple of the men weren't getting it. Dad said, "Look, you guys, I have an hour with you and I may not see you again. I am an evangelist and am called to make sure each of you has the opportunity to spend eternity with Jesus. I'm not here to play games; that's what got you into this mess." Then I saw the beauty of my Dad's ministry. The men listened to him because he'd been there. Been in their shoes, spent years in prison, and had the answer to life. We read through John 3 about being born again and two of the men confessed Jesus Christ as their Lord and Savior.

Before we left the first session, I asked the men, "How many of you came from a healthy family?" Not one raised his hand. I asked, "How many of you had a dad around who loved and cared for you?" No one raised his hand and most of them hung their heads in shame. Then I asked, "How many of you are fathers with kids at home or in protective custody?" More than half looked at me and signaled that it was true of them. Then I said, "You see this guy next to me (pointing at my dad)? He's my dad. When I was six months old he was arrested for murder. I didn't know him most of my life. He was an outlaw, abuser, and dope fiend. But I'm here tonight to tell you that God changes lives. At fifty years old he became a Christian. I gave my life to Christ and we are now fully reconciled. We've both spent a lot of time in this jail, my friends, and God is willing and able to change your life, too—from the inside out."

Several men began to weep. I continued, "Don't wait another day to begin the journey of restoration. Start trusting your heavenly Father tonight. Where our fathers messed up, God can step in. Where our dads were wounded, God brings healing. Where our dads failed, our heavenly Father prevails!" Many tears were shed and hugs of hope were shared. God moved in the hearts of the men. We had the same experience in the second session. Men gave their lives to Christ and God became their Father! He is good. All the time.

When we left the jail I couldn't stop expressing the joy I felt. I told Dad how amazing it was to fight for men together. I couldn't wait until the next time we could go together to minister to the men in jail. We drove to his house and prayed together before bed. The next morning, I was lying in bed and I heard Dad get up and build a fire. Then I heard him praying—not really sure what he was saying. He continued praying for about 15 minutes. It was too much to bear; I wept. This was my dad, truly changed and blessing others. Not the man I once knew or feared. A new creation restored into the image of what was once lost. A gentle, loving, and caring father to many in God's Kingdom. Amen.

AS IS Church

God's blessing continued as he called Gwenna and me to plant a new church called "AS IS Church." Many people seem to think they need to get their act together before they can approach Him or be part of a church. This simply is not true! God demonstrated His love for us in this: *While we were still sinners, Christ died for us* (Romans 5:8). We are committed to developing a culture of trust and acceptance as God changes people from the inside out. He is the Way, the Truth, and the Life.

I can't wait to see what the future holds with my marriage, children, family, and the AS IS Church!

fifteen

YOUR FORGIVENESS FACTOR

"Therefore, there is now no condemnation for those who are in Christ Jesus, because through Christ Jesus the law of the Spirit who gives life has set you free from the law of sin and death."
Romans 8:1, 2

Each person reading this book has a story. You matter to God, no matter where you've been or what you've done. He is waiting for you to come home. Whether you are happily married or an addict on the verge of another bender, God is patient. Whether you're a seasoned theologian or a person who's never read a page of the Bible, He waits for you to return. He loves us with an everlasting love. We have a choice.

God gives us the gift of forgiveness so we can be healthy people. He knows we need peace in our relationships. He understands that we are fallible beings who hurt each other. Forgiveness is not so much for the benefit of others, but for our own freedom.

Forgiveness is not easy and isn't meant to be. To truly forgive, we must acknowledge the pain and address the wound. We must feel to heal, there is no other way. If we don't forgive, we'll carry the past around with us like nasty, old garbage. It will sit festering, spoiling every new relationship we enter into. Each one of our families has a history with highs and lows, ups and downs, pain and joy. The path to long-term, healthy relationships is forgiveness and reconciliation.

The Forgiveness Factor is Jesus Christ. If we want to experience the abundant life found in the Kingdom of God, we must start with Him. Jesus told us, "If you have seen me, you have seen the Father." God cherishes us as His beloved children, and nothing can separate us from His love.

The question is this: will we receive it? He is willing and able to love us, but we must be receptive to His offering. He gives us the dignity of choice. It begins with understanding God's nature and who He is.

God is love. He created us in His image and longs to be our companion. He desires our affection and worship. When we choose forgiveness through Jesus Christ, He adopts us as His children.

> *"God so loved the world that He gave His one and only Son, that whoever believes in Him shall not perish, but have eternal life."*
> John 3:16

He also has a plan for each of us. When we choose to make Jesus the Lord and Savior, we can experience the abundant life. God brings clarity to confusing things in life. He provides light in the dark places. He lifts us up out of our own pitfalls and brings a newness of life. In Him, there is no darkness. He is light and life. The abundant life is a life of meaning and purpose that transcends our worldly desires.

When we begin to live as God's children, we start to see things through His eyes. The world is not such a scary place anymore. God proved His love by sending His Son, Jesus Christ. He knows our fears and our thoughts. He invites us into a personal relationship with Him.

This is not about attending church services. This is about trusting Him with our lives. Receiving Christ involves turning to God (repentance) and trusting Christ to forgive our sin. This is when God begins to transform us into who He wants us to be. Transformation takes time as we walk with Jesus.

> *"Forgiveness is me giving up my right to hurt you for hurting me."*
> Anonymous

RESOURCES

please visit
www.theforgivenessfactor.com

Pure Desire Ministries International, led by Dr. Ted Roberts and Diane Roberts, has very practical answers that deal not only with the personal shame of the struggle of sexual and other addictions, but also with the family systems that fuel the issues. Resources available include:

- *Pure Desire* by Ted Roberts
- *Pure Desire: Breakthrough & Break Free. Seven Pillars of Freedom. (Pure Desire Men's Workbook)* by Dr. Ted Roberts
- *Top Gun: Flight Manual for Young Men in a Pornified World* by Dr. Ted Roberts & Bryan Roberts
- *Betrayal & Beyond: Healing for Broken Trust* by Diane Roberts
- *Pure Desire for Women: Eight Pillars to Freedom from Love Addiction & Sexual Issues* by Diane Roberts
- *Behind the Mask: Authentic Living for Young Women* by Rebecca Bradley & Diane Roberts

Pure Desire Ministries International
Gresham, Oregon
www.puredesire.org
503-489-0230

The Genesis Process by Michael, Dye
www.genesisprocess.org

The Genesis Process will help you understand how your addictions have affected your life and relationships, and give you some basic recovery principles and practical tools to bring about biblically based life change.